Living Poor

Poor

a participant
observer
study of
choices and
priorities

BY

CAMILLE
JEFFERS

With an
introduction
By
Hylan Lewis

ANN ARBOR PUBLISHERS
610 S. Forest Avenue
Ann Arbor, Michigan 48104
665-9130

$2.50 Per Copy

living poor

A Participant Observer Study of
Priorities and Choices
by

camille jeffers

with an introduction
by

hylan lewis
howard university

ANN ARBOR PUBLISHERS

Ann Arbor, Michigan

1967

Copyright 1967
ANN ARBOR PUBLISHERS
Ann Arbor, Michigan

Library of Congress
Catalog No. 67-24378

TO MY SON

TABLE OF CONTENTS

Introduction

A respected magazine with a modest circulation recently described itself as "objective but not impartial". "Objective but not impartial" describes and also honors Camille Jeffers' *Living Poor*. This is an account of how poor parents made and lived with harsh choices and established child-rearing priorities in their own ways. It is a view of people living in poverty seen from "all points of the compass, with respect, irony, impatience and sadness", to borrow the words of the writer, Kingsley Amis. It conveys a sense of contemporary social fact and portrays enduring human truths.

This report describes some subtle as well as direct and harsh meanings of living poor today; and it also sheds light on the interplay between poverty and public housing. It should be useful to students and practitioners, and to makers of policy in health, welfare, education, housing and manpower.

During the early 1960's, Mrs. Jeffers, a staff member of the Child Rearing Study* of the Health and Welfare Council

---

*A project sponsored by the Health and Welfare Council of the National Capitol Area and supported by Mental Health Project Grants 5-R11-MH 278-5, from the National Institutes of Health, U.S. Public Health Service, Department of Health, Education and Welfare. The formal title is "Child Rearing Practices among Low Income Families in the District of Columbia"; the working title used is "Child Rearing Study."

of the National Capitol Area, lived in a public-housing project as a working mother and household head. During fifteen months as a participant observer, she shared directly and indirectly the daily routines and seasonal rhythms of a wide range of project families. She became sensitively attuned to the numerous ways in which families tried to cope with the contingencies of poverty and the many demands of living in a public-housing project.

The isolation of the public-housing projects has become progressively sharper, and invidiousness with respect to its residents has hardened since the late 1930's. Until recently, these problems of urban public housing were—or better, appeared to be—relatively independent of the forces that have created contemporary slums. Serious problems in public housing antedated by a considerable period the current general crisis of the ghetto. One of the probable effects of public housing until recent times was to delay the crisis; however, public housing in some cities is today more nearly a part of the larger urban crisis than a deterrent.

Being poor *and* living in a public-housing project makes for a "double bind"—for the families, for policy makers in social welfare and housing and for society as a whole. Any powerlessness, isolation or vulnarability to the unforeseen that characterizes the poor is highlighted in ghetto public housing. And the perverse, pathological, wasteful, threatening ways in which some respond to being poor appear more grotesque in the settings of some public-housing reservations today.*

Although public housing is sought and appreciated by many families, today it is nearly always a poignant, and often a cruel, Hobson's choice.

This report accents questions about both child-rearing practices among poor families and the social benefits of

*The studies by Lee Rainwater and associates of the Pruitt-Igoe project in St. Louis, Missouri, "Social and Community Problems in Public Housing Areas," document the accented "lower-class behavior" of some of the poor in this high-rise public housing for approximately 10,000 people. See Lee Rainwater, "Crucible of Identity: The Negro Lower-Class Family," in Talcott Parsons and Kenneth B. Clark (eds), *The Negro-American,* The Daedalus Library Volume 7, (Houghton-Mifflin Company, Boston, 1966), pp. 160-204.

public housing: (1) What characteristics and resources do families bring to a public-housing project? (2) How do family characteristics and resources affect family life and child rearing? (3) What are the selective effects of eligibility rules; and in what ways are they limiting and self-defeating—built-in incapacities? (4) How do the setting and the social organization of the housing project affect behavior and chances for growth and enlarged choices?

Indications of direct and subtle ways in which the behavior of some families was affected by the physical setting and social controls of the housing project—by site and location; the types of buildings and their distribution; demographic facts—age and sex distribution, marital status, density and morbidity; maintenance and services; management rules and practices; and the form and content of communication between management and tenants—enter naturally into this account.

An initial and continuing reaction of families living in this housing project was that of being inside a reservation or compound, literally and figuratively separated from others who are outside. Particularly telling of the sense of separation from outside, and at the same time suggesting some of the cleavages inside, was the remark of one mother who retained live hopes of "getting out": "I have been here two years, but I don't have anything to do with my neighbors. All my friends are on the outside, and that is the way I want it."

The residents of the project tended to spend inordinate amounts of time within the project; many parents were psychological captives. That many did not venture outside was not due simply to various combinations of the lack of money, the size of family, and the age of children. It had something to do with the ways in which self-consciousness and experience made them see themselves in relation to the outside and to the managers of much of their lives inside.

Among the points and propositions about living poor today that are presented and suggested in this participant-observer report, the following are likely to be particularly useful and challenging:

In the main, parents who are poor know what they want for their children and themselves. They want and prefer better food, shelter, clothing, education, more stable family unions, geared to support, and cooperative husbands and fathers; and they want the level and flow of money income that will enable them not only to get or achieve these things themselves, but that also will reduce their continuing vulnerability to little lacks—to poverty-contingencies involving food, shelter and health.

There is a pattern of social differentiation among the poor in public housing that is based more on differences in the extent to which families think they have the power or potential to change status—to escape public housing—, than it is on life styles, education and income level. This is true despite indications that small absolute differences in income can make for relatively large differences in outlook and behavior in the poor category, in as well as out of public housing.

The lack of sufficient money and its irregular flow restrict child-rearing options and force a continuous shuffling of priorities among food, shelter, clothing, health, educational, recreational and other demands.

The presumed inability of some poor parents to delay gratification is less a matter of weak will, small self-control, weak stamina or lower class norms than it is a matter of realistic and rational responses to chronic uncertainty, of conditioned reflexes related to constant vulnerability to the big and little contingencies of poverty.

"I just have to let tomorrow take care of itself" is frequently more a matter of realism based on experience than an indication of irresponsibility and of freedom from caring about self and children.

Certain aspects of the behavior of many poor are better characterized as contingency-oriented rather than present-oriented.

The most rejected and frowned-upon problem behavior of many poor parents is often less a matter of not knowing better, or of not having the ability to act differently, than it is a matter of mood; mood is critically related to the presence and absence of money with which to satisfy wants

—to exercise a minimum of self-determination.

Many of the urban poor straddle poverty and affluence. They may exhibit complex and fluctuating mixtures of the living situations and styles, possessions and tastes of different classes; and they may have linkages with relatives and friends who have "made it", or who are upwardly mobile via occupation and education.

This suggests the crucial importance of understanding the open quality and very fluid aspects of the contemporary lower middle class among urban Negroes.

To understand the influence of poverty, it is necessary to examine the expansion and shrinkage of the repertory of family roles in response to poor parents' child-rearing needs and to what is happening in the community.

There are indications that the older child in some poor families is in a particularly vulnerable position; that he is more likely to be isolated in the family and to have a less satisfactory relationship with the mother because of the relative absence of play experience, for example.

The family environment of a poor family may fluctuate markedly over relatively brief periods of child-rearing time. Opportunities for growth and development may vary markedly among children of different ages and ordinal positions; for example, speech patterns often vary markedly among children of the same family.

The lives of parents in many poor families, in and out of housing projects, are marked by extreme loneliness. The loneliness of the poor is accentuated by awareness of the lack of self-determination and of the disproportionate vulnerability to small lacks and to the unpredictable.

Families in the housing project with the most inadequate and uncertain incomes "appeared to have the most extensive communication networks in the project". They are adaptive networks, essential for survival. They facilitate the elementary exchange of small goods and services among people constantly caught with small lacks.

The shifting networks of mutual aid are pragmatic urban networks; they are not carry-overs from a rural past. They are relatively unemotional, *ad hoc* means of living now; characteristically they are not customary ways of exchange—they are not traditional claims on friendship or family.

When Mrs. Jeffers became a part of these networks she brought significant added dimensions to them. She brought the presences, the options and the resources of a resident friend from the outside. Although it was not her purpose, she was able to reduce temporarily some of the loneliness of the parents with whom she was in closest contact. She was also on occasions able to make some parents less vulnerable to small lacks. The resources she added to the pragmatic mutual-aid network were relatively small and implementing ones—transportation, information, listening ability. Importantly, she shared these antidotes to little lacks as a neighbor and as a friend—a resident link with the outside and with the world of those less vulnerable to small lacks. Acceptance, accessibility, confidence and competence in dealing with bureaucratic rules and agents, inside and outside the project (or the ghetto), are important qualities: "These are probably more important than whether a person is indigenous to the group. For some [ghetto] problems, being a local resident and having these qualities is likely to prove a boon; for others, whether a person is [indigenous] or not may not matter."

With regard to the language of the poor, this report documents that "poverty does not foster niceties of language any more than it fosters the development of social graces". And Mrs. Jeffers' experience shows that: "The problem is not one of having to speak a different language but of being willing and able to listen to what is said . . . and . . . to respond with respect and sincerity. In the Child Rearing Study, we found that is was readiness to listen and to understand that opens doors."

The aims of the Child Rearing Study of the Health and Welfare Council of the National Capitol Area were to find out how various kinds of low-income families cope with the problems of child rearing and to discover what kinds of improvement programs are practicable. Materials were collected as well as participant observations in a variety of settings.

Participant observers for the Child Rearing Study, in addition to Mrs. Jeffers, were Richard Slobodin, an anthropologist who studied a one-block enclave during a summer; Roscoe Lewis, a sociologist, who lived in a blighted section of the inner city over a three-month period; Elliot Liebow, an anthropologist, who studied street-corner men during more than a year as a CRS staff member; and William Watson, a social worker and street-gang expert, who also studied street-corner men as a participant observer over a period of several months. Mrs. Jeffers was unique not only for the length of time she lived in the housing project, but also because she doubled in brass as a participant observer. Her main assignment in the beginning was to observe and interview families in the field. She later served as assistant director of the project.

I, as director of the Child Rearing Study, and Mrs. Jeffers, as author of this report for the study, wish to acknowledge especially an indebtedness to two key people— Mr. Isadore Seeman, executive director of the Health and Welfare Council of the National Capitol Area, and Mr. Walter Washington, formerly executive director of the National Capitol Housing Authority, and now Chairman of the New York Housing Authority. Each extended full cooperation, a free hand and confidence. And each showed the keenest appreciation of what social-science methods and findings might contribute to enlightened social policy and to better management of services in housing, health and welfare.

The responsibility for the document presented here is solely that of the project director and the author. Maximum efforts have been made to protect the privacy and anonymity of all persons by changes in names; and by shuffling of places and sequences in instances where they were not essential to the account.

Hylan Lewis
Howard University
December 28, 1966

I

ENTERING PUBLIC HOUSING, 1960

The Purpose

"How would you like to live in a public housing project?"
This is the question that greeted me when I answered a long
distance telephone call from my prospective employer, the
director of a study of child-rearing behavior among low-income families in Washington, D.C.* Momentarily startled,
I could only think to ask if he was serious, knowing, of
course, that he was. I was being hired for intensive family
interviewing, and living in a public-housing project had been
one of the several ways we had discussed of observing low-
income families at first hand. I had indicated in an earlier
conversation that I was not averse to considering such an
experience for my four-year-old son and me. At the time the

* A five-year project, sponsored by the Health and Welfare Council
of the National Capitol Area, and supported by Mental Health Project
Grants, 5-R11-MH 278-5, from the National Institutes of Health,
U.S. Public Health Service, Department of Health, Education, and
Welfare. The operating title is "Child Rearing Practices Among
Low Income Families in the District of Columbia."

In this and other reports, it is referred to as the Child Rearing
Study (CRS).

likelihood had seemed remote, but, when the Child Rearing Study director told me that the necessary arrangements were being made, it was clear that the remote was closer at hand.

The blurted question with which I had responded was my way of gaining time to shift into the new gear required. Shifting these psychological gears was really not hard—I already had a strong conviction that, given the goals of the Child Rearing Study, probably the best way to learn about people was to live with them. My conviction that I could carry out such an assignment was strengthened by the belief that my social work training and more than twenty years of experience would help me maintain objectivity, develop rapport with the residents, and discipline myself to write the full and regular field reports required. I felt, too, that the timing was propitious from a personal point of view, since I would be leaving one community in which I had ties for another in which I had practically no ties. I would have a minimum of carry-over from one life into another, and there would be little need to reconcile two lives.

In the planning stage, considerable thought was given to the nature of my tenancy. I was to be a rent-paying tenant subject to all tenant rules and regulations. My basic task was to gain acceptance and to participate in the on-going life of the project so that I might observe, experience, and interpret some of the family and community influences on child rearing among the residents of a public-housing project, a segment of the population that is by definition low income.

Although no attempt was to be made to disguise my identity or conceal my employment with the Health and Welfare Council, my residence was to be as unobtrusive as possible; I was to be just another tenant going about her normal business. Wherever and whenever an explanation about my work seemed called for, I was to explain that my job was to get a better understanding of current family practices and of some of the problems today's parents experience in bringing up children. The study director and I believed that if I were successful in maintaining this posture and candor, people would learn to accept me and my child and overlook my role of observer. I, in turn, would become more practiced in understanding and sharing the experiences and perspectives of public-housing tenants.

My assignment was to last for a minimum of one year and was to supplement the intensive family interviewing and observations to be done by the Child Rearing Study project in other parts of the city. Since I was also heavily involved in these other Study tasks, this meant that I would be a participant observer at the housing project primarily during evenings and weekends. While this apportionment of time was largely dictated by other Study demands, it undoubtedly provided some advantage in that my daily routine was identifiable with that of other working mothers in the project.

Some Reactions, Expected and Unexpected

Living in a public housing project was not a new experience for me. In the late 1930's, while apartment hunting, I had lived for several weeks with friends in New York City's Harlem River Houses. In those days, I had many friends living in Harlem River Houses since just about everybody I knew had a low income. At that time, public housing was much sought after by the young families I knew who were trying to pull themselves out of the Depression. The monthly, project rental fees of twenty to thirty dollars contrasted sharply with the exorbitant rental charges of fifty-five to sixty-five dollars for a four-room apartment in a privately-owned building. Many who paid those high rentals eked them out of incomes of twelve- to fifteen-hundred dollars a year; as a consequence, many young families were forced either to share an apartment or have roomers. To get into a housing project was, understandably, the goal of quite a few white-collar, as well as blue-collar, families. Nowhere was there a better break in housing costs.

By 1960, however, the image, the aura and some of the functions of public housing had changed markedly. My voluntary decision to live in a public-housing project occasioned raised eyebrows among friends and acquaintances, Negro and white. The reactions I encountered provided a telling

3

commentary on the gap between those who live in private housing and those who through limited choice or no choice at all, live in public housing today.

To some people, my decision to live in a public-housing project smacked of unfair labor practices, an agreement extracted as a condition of my employment on the Child Rearing Study staff. Others considered the arrangement a reflection of my eccentricity. Certain skeptics conveyed their doubts by politely inquiring, "Do you really think you will like it?" The more class conscious wondered aloud, "Isn't there some other way?" or said bluntly, "I don't see why you want to live with those people."

The existence of a "social difference" greater than and different from class differences was suggested in varying versions of the "How perfectly fascinating!" comment, as though I were going on a safari to some distant, exotic land. The sharpest comment, and the one which most surprised me, was the indictment carried in the recurrent question, "Well, it might be all right for you, but what about your child?"

During the Depression and probably as recently as the 1940's, many people could identify their counterparts in public housing and might even envy them to some degree. Recent developments have apparently walled off those who live in public housing from those who do not. Whether these walls are economic, social psychological, cultural or just plain brick and mortar, it is important to look behind them. Some of what I saw, heard, thought, felt and learned during my 15 month's stay on the public-housing side of the wall is the subject of this report.

My Family and My Home

There were two other members in my family beside myself. My four-year old son, Richard,* was an outgoing youngster whose ready response to play helped him make his way into any group. My twenty-two-year old friend, Helen, came to Washington with me to attend business school. She had lived in a public-housing project in her na-

* Fictitious names for practically all persons, institutions, and locations have been substituted throughout this report.

4

tive southern community with her widowed mother, sisters and brothers. Since this was her first extended trip away from home, her tendency was to regard me as a mother substitute, and I was old enough to be just that.

Initially, I had some concern that the differences in our physical appearances and surnames might raise some questions, but, quite early in our stay, this concern was allayed when Helen reported that she had been asked if I had raised her. I realized that we presented an acceptable image; a "taken-in" child is hardly an oddity among low- and middle-income Negro families. Having Helen with me proved to be an asset, as some of the contacts she developed extended my knowledge and mobility and deepened my insight.

My household's daily routine was well established by the time we moved into the project three months after our arrival in Washington. Helen left home in time for 8:00 a.m. classes at school and returned home at 4:00 p.m.; I took my son back and forth to nursery school on my way to and from work. This pattern continued while we were in the project.

The two-bedroom apartment assigned to us overlooked a large court landscaped with shrubbery, trees, and grass plots. The wide walks of the area afforded ample room for tricycles and wagons. Long stone benches in strategic spots provided gathering places for visitors to the court. A fenced-off, barren playground for the children, however, was seldom used.

Pleased as I was with our newly-decorated apartment, I was even more pleased with its location—a good vantage point for some unobserved observing. I could watch the court to see who was there and time my trips accordingly to that outside gathering spot.

Moving-In Day

Moving-in day started with a cool, sunny morning. Helen and Richard followed their usual school routines while I rushed to meet the movers at eight in the morning at the project. Perhaps due to the early hour and brisk weather, there were no bystanders. Tenants who did go in and out of the building politely walked around the movers and paid little attention to my arrival. As the moving men came and went, complaining of how long they had to wait for the elevator and the consequent long climb up the stairs, I remained in the apartment supervising the placement of the furniture. Occasionally, I stood at the door waiting for the next load and hoping to get a glimpse of neighbors, but the rows of apartment doors remained closed.

I waited a couple of days for some sign of recognition from my immediate neighbors, but their doors still remained closed. My eagerness for some sign of recognition doubtless resulted from my desire to relieve some of my unshakable anxiety about intruding into other people's lives. How would they react to me? Would they feel I did not belong? What would they think of the reason I was there? I became preoccupied with the explanation I would give for being there and spent my first few days polishing and repolishing various versions. But no one asked for my explanation. I soon realized that people were much less concerned about me than I was about them.

Deciding that the first move was apparently up to me, I used the fact that there were no ice trays in my refrigerator as an excuse to establish direct contact with some one of my neighbors. I ventured down the hall and tapped lightly on an apartment door. The young woman who opened the door regarded me impassively, as she looked down upon me from her greater height and waited for me to speak. Explaining my predicament, I asked if she could spare some ice cubes.

"I don't have no ice cubes," she replied, curt and unsmiling. I must have registered some disbelief, for she added with finality, "I use my freezer for storage and only make ice cubes in the summer." Hoping to circumvent her dismissal, I quickly pointed to another apartment, asking if she thought I should try there.

"They're not there," was her laconic reply. "They're away." When I nodded toward another apartment, I was rebuffed again. "She don't have any either; she do the same thing I do."

When I pressed for some alternative, she suggested the superintendent but gave me directions to his apartment only when I asked for them. Her manner never changed, and she spoke in flat, dry tones. There was nothing to indicate that my problem was of the least concern to her. Yet, as I turned to go to the superintendent's apartment she called after me, "I'll make some for you tomorrow."

This was the beginning of my association with Mrs. Todd, a 23-year-old mother of four young children. It was an association that, in time, became not only daily but close.

"The Girls" and the Court

As I sized up the court from my window during those first weeks, I noticed that there were two major groupings, one of older women and one of younger women. Each group regularly gravitated to certain benches. Occasionally, there was some intermingling of members of each group, but, by and large, the differing age groups remained separate. The group of older women was smaller in number, seldom more than five or six, and more stable in its composition. The younger group was larger and had a more fluid constituency, but I was soon able to pick out some of the regulars. I decided to make my debut in the court with the older women—for one thing, I was more readily identifiable with them because of my gray hair.

I had noticed that one of the older women, Mrs. Harris, was usually first in the court in the late afternoon. Immaculate in her starched house dress, her bluish-gray hair secured by a hairnet, she settled herself on the pillow she brought for the stone bench and waited for her companions to arrive. Seeing her alone one day, I hurried down to the court with my son and his tricycle. I started him off playing and headed toward Mrs. Harris. She was immediately responsive.

"That your boy?" she asked without hesitation. When I responded affirmatively, she continued, "Is that all you got?" She seemed surprised at my acknowledgement that I had but one child, and, speaking of her fondness for her two grandchildren, said reflectively, "I never knew I would have so much gold and diamonds in my old age." Then she let me know I was not the only unobserved observer; she had watched me move in.

As other women joined us and began talking, no one bothered to introduce herself or ask my name, but I was readily included in conversations. They soon became The Girls to me since they would often use this term in inquiring about absent members of the group.

Mrs. Harris, whom I came to regard as the dowager queen of the court, was in her seventies. She had been widowed after a long and happy marriage about which she loved to reminisce. She lived proudly on her social-security benefits and commanded the respect of young and old. She had been one of the first tenants in the building and knew many of the young mothers by their first names. Intensely interested in children, she did not hesitate to chide some of the mothers about their child-rearing behavior. Once I thought she had erred in challenging an outspoken young mother, Mrs. Martin, who was scolding and slapping her baby for picking at its nose. In a stern but friendly manner, Mrs. Harris said to her: "Leave that baby alone before I hit you up side the head!" Pouting a little but without a word, Mrs. Martin stopped. It was the only time I ever saw anyone make Mrs. Martin hold her tongue.

Another one of The Girls was Mrs. Ferguson. Her sprightliness belied her 80-odd years, and she was as ready as a young girl to go on a boat ride or a fishing trip. An active person who seemed to be on the go a great deal of the time, she kept a sharp eye on the court and the events of the day. She knew who had been taken away in an ambulance, why a squad car was parked outside and who had just moved out. Sometimes she would have her facts wrong, but The Girls were understanding and attributed this to her age. However, they were mindful of the fact that it was best not to say anything in Mrs. Ferguson's presence that they did not want repeated.

A third member of the group was Mrs. Doyle, a tall, thin, white woman in her sixties who palled with Mrs. Ferguson. Wrinkled and toothless, she described herself as having been a "good looker" in her day, and traces of her good looks remained. She had been illiterate when she came to this country and she was extremely proud of the way she had taught herself to read and write and of the responsible jobs she had been able to hold as a result. In her lively moods, she would regale us with jokes from the extensive repertoire she had developed in her younger days when she was a party-goer. At other times, she would complain bitterly about the crabbiness of her ailing husband and wish she could realize her lifelong dream to live by herself in a house on a hill.

Mrs. Taylor, a stout woman who occasionally joked about her size, was also in her sixties and lived on Old Age Assistance with her invalid husband. There was a warmth in her personality that attracted children and they could often be found hovering around her. While sitting in the court she was always solicitous about their welfare, calling to them to be careful or not to run too fast. Sometimes, when the ice cream wagon pulled up, she would reach into her coin purse and take out a dime to give to a child (sometimes my son) who was looking longingly at the other children licking their Popsicles. Once when I remarked that she acted like a doting grandmother, she responded to my surprise, "I can't be a grandmother as I ain't never had no children of my own."

Mrs. Jordan, a short and squat white woman, who appeared to be near 70, first attracted my attention when I saw her sitting in the court on quite cool days in a sleeveless dress. She attributed her hardiness to the fact that she was practically raised on the water on Maryland's Eastern Shore. Partially deaf, she sometimes just sat contentedly in the group; at other times, she would join in the conversation, especially when the group was small. Always smiling and pleasant, she seemed at peace with herself and her surroundings. Even her daughter from Arizona, who visited her while I was at the project, could not entice Mrs. Jordan to Arizona for a visit. As far as Mrs. Jordan was concerned, a bus or train trip would be too long, and she dismissed her daughter's offer of a plane trip with a skyward glance, saying, "I haven't lost anything up there!"

These were some of The Girls with whom I spent many an hour in the court, listening to their aches and pains, their criticisms of the child-rearing behavior of the younger women, their reminiscences of their younger days, and their discussions about sex.

Visits to Two Neighborhood Churches

In addition to making contacts with individual families and the groups in the court, I started attending services of two of the churches in the immediate neighborhood. One church was connected with a small orthodox denomination; the other was a "Holiness" church which, in the span of ten years, had developed from a store-front church to an imposing edifice with branches in several cities. I began as an ordinary church-goer, making no effort to establish contact with the ministers. While occasional glances in my direction indicated that my presence was noticed, I was given no special recognition other than that normally given to visitors.

After attending the smaller church for several Sundays, I shifted to the Holiness church for a while. However, my absence from the first church did not go unnoticed; in a few weeks, I received an unexpected visit from the Reverend Mr. Nelson, the minister, who called me "Sis" as he did the women in his church. Having obtained my address from the visitors' book I had signed, he had ostensibly come to find out why I had stopped attending his church. I seized this opportunity to explain in detail the nature of my assignment and why I had not been to his church recently.

"I thought you were up to something, Sis," he said when I concluded. "I could see that you were a professional person, but I thought I would wait to see what it was because you know how women are—you just can't come out and ask them things!"

Encouraged by my explanation, the Reverend Mr. Nelson said that my purpose fitted right in with what he had in mind. He had more children in his Sunday school than members in his church, because many of the parents retained their membership in the churches in their former neighborhoods but sent their children to his Sunday school. He was concerned about the children and wanted to do more for them. His hope was that I would join his church whereupon

10

he would appoint me assistant Sunday school superintendent to develop a program of Christian education for the
children in his church and in the neighborhood since he felt
that his goals and the goals of the Child Rearing Study were
similar. He indicated that there would be latitude for me to
do whatever I wanted and what I could to involve both
parents and children in the church project.* Stressing the
dearth of leadership in so many neighborhoods, he insisted,
"We need people like you."

Another request to join in church activities came from
one of the stalwarts of the Holiness church, Mrs. Cartwright.
She was an extremely articulate woman in her sixties with
whom I struck up a conversation when I stayed for a church
dinner after one of the Sunday services. Subsequently, I
brought her some discarded toys for the nursery she managed during Sunday services, and we became quite friendly.
Having joined the church only four years earlier, Mrs. Cartwright devoted much of her spare time attending to all of its
many activities. "I haven't been in the right place until I
came here," she said, complaining of the fact that in the
orthodox denomination to which she formerly belonged,
she was helping make paper costumes for plays and entertainment "every time I turned around". She had not made
a paper costume since she had been in this church. Instead,
the pastor's emphasis was on learning what the Bible meant,
and that was the way she thought it should be.

When I expressed appreciation of the sermons that I had
heard and mentioned my surprise that they were so related
to everyday living, she commented, "That's just what I
mean. I wish you would come into this church. We need
people like you. I know the Lord has something for you to do
here. People will say, 'If she sees something to it, there
must be something in it!'"

Mrs. Cartwright felt that her minister had a healing power
and possessed the kind of personality that "draws people".

* This offer was a temptation in view of our action-oriented research
plans. However, it had to be refused not only because of the current
demands on my time, but also because the Study's time schedule
meant that it was unready to take on an action program at such
an early stage.

11

A semi-invalid woman whom I met in the church spoke of the "pulling power" of the church. An elderly gentleman, who had been with the church since its inception, said, "It's the people. When people get the Holy Ghost, they are just different. I love to associate with them."

I was struck by the fact that the church attracted a large number of men, young and old, many of whom gravitated to seats in what seemed to be the men's side of the church. Often the minister would direct his remarks to them. I sensed an intimate, personal connection between him and his congregation.

At the risk of doing injustice to one of his sermons, I have paraphrased it. It was an eloquently didactic discourse on child rearing and parental responsibility. The text was from Deuteronomy 32:11:

> As an eagle stirreth her nest, fluttereth over her young, spreadeth abroad her wings, taketh them on her wings.

The minister likened the eagle to parents and defined in elaborate detail the way the eagle picks its spot to build its nest high out of reach, giving much more attention to its choice than "some of you people do".

> Next the eagle sees that his nest is well made. He carefully builds a good foundation—"better than some of you've got"—and mends all the weak places. Then the eagle sits on her eggs—" never more than three"—until they are hatched.

> The eagle feeds her young, goes out and catches food for them. She doesn't let her children starve like some people do who let their children come up with rickets. She is not like parents who don't feed their children but always feed themselves.

> When the eaglets begin to sprout feathers, the mother lets them walk out a little around the nest—but "never out of sight." She is not like some people who pay no attention to where their children are.

"Any child not in school should be working. The mother works, the father works, and they're sitting at home waiting for you to put something in their mouths! You send them to be educated in college and they are worse fools than when, they started. 'I want to be a teacher, I want to be a lawyer,' is all they say. Ain't nothing wrong with being a good ditch digger. This church wouldn't be here if we didn't have some good ditch diggers."

"Some of you are more concerned if your bulldog disappears. In no time you are out in the street asking, 'Have you seen my dog?' You worry to death about your dog, but if your children are out until twelve and one o'clock in the morning, you don't think to ask nobody. You go to bed and have two or three dreams and still don't think to ask about your children."

When the eaglets have enough feathers to learn to fly, the mother puts thorns in the nest so that they can't sit down. They have to learn to fly.
Then when the eagle feels it's time for the eaglet to learn to fly, he sweeps it off the limb. Down, down goes the eaglet and the mother sweeps down below it, spreading her wings to catch the learner. She does this again and again until the bird learns to fly, but the mother is always there to catch it. This is what parents have to do. Some of them don't put thorns in the nest to make their children get up and learn to be on their own or give them the help they need when they do try to be on their own.

Calling this part of the sermon the "natural comparison", the minister concluded with a "spiritual comparison", "The eagle is God and we are His young; God spreads His wings and when we falter He is there to pick us up.

The Scope of Participant Observation

The first few months passed quickly, and it became

evident that my problem was not going to be that of gaining acceptance. The first person in the project who verbally expressed acceptance of me and my work was Mr. Shorter, an affable man in his thirties with several children in his family. Our acquaintance had developed around ice cubes, laundry room keys, car troubles and the upkeep of the grounds. After one of our conversations, he asked quizzically, "Just what do you do, anyway?" When I told him about the Child Rearing Study, he said, "I thought it must be something like that. There's just something different about you." I indicated my interest in talking with him about his experiences in bringing up children, and he readily granted my request.

Mrs. Harris had a different approach. All she wanted to know was where I worked, and as soon as I answered "Health and Welfare Council," she responded approvingly, "Oh, you're on Civil Service."*

When I eventually began to ask some mothers for information and thoughts about their experiences in bringing up their children, I felt that the cooperative responses were based more on our personal relationships than on their interest in being part of the Study.

Mrs. Todd, the neighbor who made the ice cubes for me, was perhaps the person who showed most openly her complete understanding of my purpose. One day she brought over a record she had borrowed for me to hear and we listened to it on the spot. Entitled "Outside", it was a hilarious Shelley Berman take-off on a psychiatrist answering parents' questions on child rearing. Noting my enjoyment of the record, Mrs. Todd dryly commented, "I thought you would like it."

From the beginning of my residence, the primary goal was to obtain intensive and continuing pictures of a selected number of people and situations rather than a superficial coverage of a large number of persons and aspects of life in the public-housing project. The receptiveness I found in

* In this instance, as in the instance of other persons, both inside and outside of the project, Mrs. Harris was obviously confusing the Health and Welfare Council with the U.S. Department of Health, Education, and Welfare.

these first few months made me realize that the real problem was going to be one of not overextending myself. However, even when limits were imposed, my activities as a resident mother were many and varied. During those first few months, I chatted in the court with The Girls and the young mothers; visited with neighbors and went to the homes of some of their relatives; took trips to nearby beaches, the zoo and parks; attended a dance, a funeral, Sunday church services, midweek prayer meetings, gospel singing concerts and a church youth convention; and wrote field notes.

These activities of the first few months did much to set and shape the next year's patterns of living with my fellow tenants, neighbors and friends.

II

MY NEIGHBORS AND FRIENDS

Some Family Types and Variations Among Tenants

My neighbors proved to be a heterogeneous group. They included young and old parents and their families. Negro families were predominant, but there was a scattering of white households. A large proportion of Negroes were young parents in their twenties with two to four children, often all of preschool age. The high-school graduate was not uncommon among these parents and many had had some high school training. Not infrequently, the schooling of the young parents had been interrupted by pregnancy and marriage. Most of the white families I knew were in the 30 to 40 age range, and the one-child family was more apt to be found among this group. The elderly population consisted of widows, widowers and couples—often a wife with an invalid or semi-invalid husband.

I began to identify three types of families among my

neighbors and fellow tenants. The dividing lines were not always clear cut, and there were gradations in between these crude categories.

There was one group of families that divorced themselves and their children from project life as completely as they could. One such mother told me, "I have been here two years, but I don't have anything to do with my neighbors. All my friends are on the outside, and that is the way I want it." These families frequently disapproved of most of their neighbors and permitted their children to play only with the children of one or two acquaintances in the project. They tended to live behind closed doors. When a mother from this category made a rare visit into the court, perhaps to escape the summer heat of her apartment, she would generally sit apart from the already-formed cluster of mothers. The husband, sometimes a high-school graduate, usually had some degree of job security and gave many indications that he was satisfactorily playing his part as husband and father. The children of these parents appeared well cared for, and the parents both said and demonstrated that they wanted to do their best for them. One mother in this category based her need and plan to control her family size on this wish for her children. She said, "Two is all I can see and do the things I want for them."

Families in this category were striving to get ahead. They regarded public housing as a temporary expedient; they had no desire or plans to stay. They were geared toward moving up into rental of private housing and eventually into home ownership in one of the "better neighborhoods".

My neighbors, the Caldwells, fitted this rough characterization. Mr. Caldwell, a young man in his twenties, had a white-collar, civil-service job. Always well-groomed, he was courteous, poised in bearing, but aloof. His petite wife, who could easily have been mistaken for a teenager, was shy and retiring. Obviously devoted to her three small children, she hovered protectively nearby when she took them to play or when she took them into the court while she used the facilities in the nearby laundry room.

Their children were generally spotlessly clean and seemed well disciplined. Sometimes Mr. Caldwell could be seen after work taking them for a walk or taking them and his wife for a ride in his 1953 Ford.

There was an air of self-sufficiency about the Caldwells. In the time I was in the project, the only tenant I knew that I saw visit them was the superintendent, Mr. Shorter. He went to see the hi-fi set that Mr. Caldwell had built. In their togetherness and in their behavior, the Caldwells were a reasonable facsimile of the conventional picture of the young, alert, American working man's family that is, hopefully, upwardly mobile.

Less educated than Mr. Caldwell, but also maintaining some aloofness from the other tenants, was Mr. Gibbons, a man in his forties. He described himself as living "very quietly" with his wife and teen-age daughter. While he pridefully commented, "Nobody has been in our house since we've lived here," he still maintained friendlier relations with his neighbors than did Mr. Caldwell. Mr. Gibbons could be counted on to take someone willingly for surplus food or for an emergency trip to D.C. General Hospital in his battered old Plymouth.

Mr. Gibbons considered himself a captive of the housing project, since his wife had moved there during his lengthy hospitalization for a back injury that had occurred on his job.

His one desire was to get well enough to return to work on a full-time basis so that he could leave the housing project. He had been paying $19 more a month for rent before he moved into the project; he was sorry that they had had to give up their apartment. There, he said, he could do as he pleased.

A second gross category of families included those couples that differed from the Caldwells not so much in their orientation to the present and future, as in their dispositions not to dissociate themselves so completely from most of their neighbors. For example, they might associate with classmates whom they knew prior to living in the project, or with acquaintances met as a result of the wives' participation in the Recreation Department's preschool program or the husbands' participation in the athletic activities of the Recreation Department. More characteristically, they might be friendly with one or two of their immediate neighbors with whom they had developed mutual-assistance arrangements.

The husbands' employment ranged from the stable to the unstable, and life for these families was a little more precarious than for those in the first category. They permitted their children more freedom than families like the Caldwells but still maintained considerable supervision over them. Parents in this group planned less explicitly for the futures of their children and were more preoccupied with their day-to-day physical care.

The Queenes were in this category. Mr. Queene was in his late twenties and had come from his home town in a neighboring state with less than a fifth-grade education. He was steadily employed in a garage and was making $75 a week; he had had a recent raise. Mrs. Queene had a tenth-grade education. Generally immaculate herself, she doted on dressing her two children well. In fact, they were the best dressed of the children who frequented the court. She was active in the preschool mothers' club and had several fast friends throughout the building. Mr. Queene, an outgoing person, played an important part on the baseball team of the recreation center. He had prevailed upon his wife to move into the project against her better judgment for she had thought it was going to be too expensive. Her prediction had been correct. She had had to take a larger apartment than she wanted, and the rent went up whenever Mr. Queene got a raise. She preferred to live in private housing elsewhere in the city.

Another family in this category was the Norrises. Mr. Norris, a dapper 40-year-old man, was approximately 15 years older than his wife. I would see him come home in the evenings carrying bags of groceries, and, just as regularly, I would see him leave the house after he had eaten dinner and sit on the curb where some of the men gathered. He was a truck driver who was unemployed for several weeks during the year. His repeated failure to find work over a span of time was undoubtedly behind the fact that on one occasion, he came shamefacedly to my door to borrow a car token.

Unlike Mr. Caldwell, Mr. Norris and Mr. Queene seemed to regard child care as primarily their wives' responsibility; their responsibility as husbands was to work and to support their families. Mrs. Norris, a junior-high-school dropout, was immersed in the problems of physical care of their three preschool children and resented her husband's failure to help.

The third rough category of families that I distinguished appeared to have the most extensive communication network in the project. This group included some one-parent families and families with the most inadequate and uncertain incomes; the task of keeping a roof over their heads and food in their children's mouths occupied much of their time. They seemed to know people on every floor. Characteristically, their associations were tenuous and shifting, based largely on their shared needs for various kinds of help in child rearing and running a household, including baby sitting. Lack of funds affected their mobility and independence in such ways, it seemed, that inordinate amounts of their lives had had to be built around, or confined to, the housing project.

Their children had more freedom of movement outside the home than did children in the other two categories. As early as their second or third years, children from this third group of parents could be seen outside playing alone without adult supervision but, supposedly, under the watchful eye of a brother or a sister not much older than themselves.

Mrs. Todd, the neighbor who made the ice cubes for me after that first noncommittal dialogue, was in this group. She did not relish the task of having sole responsibility for four children while her husband was away on Navy duty. Some of her discontent appeared to reflect itself in her uneven handling of the children.

My first impression was that she had many friends in the project; this erroneous impression was corrected when most of them proved to be transient acquaintances. She maintained sustained contacts with only two people during the 15 months I was there. One continuing association was with a high-school friend, who lived on another floor, and the other was with our mutual neighbor, Mrs. Norris.

Mrs. Todd had grown up in the area and was anxious to leave, saying, "There are still the same old wineheads standing on the street corners; only difference now is that they're older." She preferred to be overseas with her husband, but, that failing, she wanted to be in a housing project nearer the servicemen's commissary where she could buy food more cheaply.

Also in this group was 24-year-old Mrs. Martin, the outspoken young woman whom Mrs. Harris, a senior member of The Girls, had silenced. Mrs. Martin had separated from her husband after the birth of their third child. Because he did not support the family the way she thought he should, she had asked him to leave. His irregular payments of court-ordered support kept her budget unbalanced, and she was constantly trying to make ends meet on her supplemental public-assistance grant. Her fourth child, an infant girl, was illegitimate; this child's father contributed regularly to her support and was intensely interested in her.

Mrs. Martin's children, all under five, had the run of the project. Always ready to battle for her children, Mrs. Martin treated them with a mixture of harshness and affection that the children seemed to understand and anticipate.

Pragmatic Mutual Aid

All of these families knew each other; however, their styles of, and occasions for, association differed. Mrs. Norris and Mrs. Todd were more friendly with each other than with anyone else, as were Mrs. Queene and Mrs. Martin. Everyone liked Mr. Gibbons, but no one maintained much contact with his wife who kept to herself. Mrs. Caldwell was pleasant when she met her neighbors in the hallways, but spent little or no time in their company. Her husband was reputed to have been friendly with Mr. Todd before he went on Navy duty, since both had known each other before graduation from the same high school. Although quite a few of the tenants had lived in the neighborhood and attended school together, they maintained a checkerboard pattern of friendships. I never got any sense of a widespread and continuing cohesive group in the housing project. Nor did I sense strong identification with the neighborhood and community among the residents I knew.

Many friendships and informal groupings among mothers were related to the need for mutual assistance in child care and household management. Some of these relationships had a temporary, make-shift character, growing out of baby-sitting needs, for example. In many instances, the persons with whom a mother was the most friendly were the ones with whom she exchanged services. The needs for such baby-sitting services were common to most of the mothers who would leave their small children with neighbors while they made clinic visits or shopping trips, went to work or enjoyed a night out.

The unspoken theme of this kind of mutual aid was: "You take care of mine, and I'll take care of yours." A mother with three, four or more children frequently found it useful to develop more than one such connection. Some mothers had three or four persons upon whom they could call in an emergency and often distributed their children among them to avoid overburdening any one woman.

It was impressive to see how quickly some mothers could parcel out their children and just as impressive to see the way some neighbors would rise to the occasion when such demands were made. For example, when Mrs. Martin had to undergo emergency hospitalization for a few days, some friends of hers, who already had three children of their own, took in Mrs. Martin's children. The wife cared for them during the day and the husband slept in the apartment with the children at night.

Sometimes an informal barter system developed when mothers did not require or could not reciprocate with the same service, but could render some other service for which there was a demand. For example, Mrs. Todd, who had skill as a hairdresser, would often set hair in exchange for baby-sitting services.

Mutual assistance with household management tasks and problems was primarily related to borrowing a wide variety of household goods. The things I was called on to do as a neighbor and friend gave insight into the problems that some of the families faced. Items borrowed from me included boys' clothing; medical supplies such as aspirin, calomine lotion, cough syrup and bandages; housekeeping supplies and equipment, including cleansers, soap powders, mops, pails, vacuum cleaner, floor wax, iron and ironing board; and food, generally staples. Returnable items were brought back, and, with expendable items, the borrowers always expressed the intent to repay me in the future— in kind or in some other way.

One might think that the most frequent request for a loan was for money but this was not true in my experience. Usually the mothers did not ask each other for money loans. In most instances it would have been futile, or nearly so, since money was the scarcest basic commodity. A request for carfare, for example, was more likely to be phrased as a request for a car token; a lender might have no money but still might have a week's supply of car tokens. Sometimes laundry tokens were borrowed for the laundry room. Rather than attempt to borrow money for food, mothers were apt to ask for a specific item of food. Often this was bread, borrowed in slices, not loaves. Sometimes it was a cup of sugar, a cup of flour or an egg. It could even be a dash of salt, pepper or cinnamon.

One of the reasons that no one expected to find much money in circulation, particularly among people who lived on semi-monthly and monthly incomes, was that the general practice was to pay bills and stock up on food as soon as the money came in. In a few days the money was gone, and there was little or no cash on hand until the next check.

Part of the meaning of the scarcity of money was etched in my mind by a remark Mrs. Todd made one day when I handed her a dollar which a man had left with me to pay her for doing his wife's hair. Mrs. Todd, who lived on a serviceman's allotment, looked ruefully at the crumpled bill and said, "Looks like something is wrong with this. It looks so small. I haven't seen money for so long that it looks like it's shrunk!"

Household Furnishings

The apartments in the building were cheerful and bright

with windows in every room except in some of the bathrooms, a circumstance that was particularly disconcerting to Mrs. Todd who dryly commented, "Whoever heard of a bathroom with no window in it!" She could no more accept the ventilator in the bathroom as an adequate substitute for a window than she could accept the fact that her expectation of a bathroom shower had been disappointed. Undeterred, she bought a shower curtain anyway and put it up.

There were many cupboards in the kitchen and closets in every room. However, my pleasure at having so much storage space for my accumulations was not shared by all the tenants. "What do they expect you to put in all them cupboards?" one mother asked. And as I began to see open cupboards with little food and few dishes, linen closets with no linen, and clothes closets sparsely hung with clothing, I realized that low incomes do not permit much, if any, accumulation. Thus, clothes closets became broom closets and were sometimes used as a place for drying clothes, a pervasive need.

The floors in all of the rooms were a mottled green and black tile. Although I occasionally caught a glimpse of linoleum on living room floors as I passed open doors, the young families I knew disliked the use of linoleum and identified it with their elders. Their preference was for highly polished floors and scatter rugs. Sometimes they called upon an old gentleman in the building who had a floor polisher to do their floors for them, and he seemed to enjoy rendering this service, whether or not the women could afford to pay.

An item which was much prized but appeared infrequently was a full-sized rug. The rugs on the floor of my apartment drew the most comments from visitors. When a visiting mother said with a sigh, "Some day I'm going to have a rug," I realized that much that many take for granted was beyond the horizon of the low-income family. Often the most that these mothers could afford were cotton scatter rugs. One mother's finishing touch in preparing her home for the return of her husband from military service was to borrow for a few weeks a nine-by-twelve cotton rug from a friend.

Among the young families who were just acquiring furniture, the tastes in furnishings were conventional modern matched suites, picture window lamps, pole lamps, coffee tables, dinette sets (rather than kitchen tables and chairs), and colored telephones.* Sometimes a portable bar was to be seen. Most families had a large-screen television, and some families owned a combination television and record player. The latest interest was in the acquisition of a hi-fi, generally of the portable variety. A number of the families had washing machines. While a particular apartment might not have all of these items, most of those I saw had enough to suggest the occupants' awareness of vogues and standards in furnishings.

Many families were preoccupied with fixing up their homes. A favorite pastime of mothers was visiting back and forth to see each other's latest purchases, not without some evidence of competition. Color schemes were emphasized and attempts were made to achieve dramatic effects. Drapes in the winter were exchanged for cottage curtains in the summer when these could be afforded.

The quantity and quality of the furniture was one of the features that distinguished one household from another. Many purchases were made on the installment plan; as Mrs. Todd put it, "Everybody buys from the three H's—Hahn's, Hub, and Hecht's." Families would characteristically buy goods on the basis of the amount of the monthly payment or payments that they could handle. In many instances, they would have to complete payments on one set of items before starting payments on the next purchases. Conversations about furnishings suggested that many families generally had well in mind what their next purchases were going to be after they had finished with the current ones. Occasionally I would see a delivery truck unloading a new, but insubstantial looking piece of furniture, and would have doubts as to whether it would last until it was paid for.

The problem of trying to furnish a house out of scant funds had some effect on people's attitudes towards apartment size. Because of the sex difference of her two children, Mrs. Queene, for example, was required by project regula-

---

* Colored telephones were among the cheapest and most easily-attainable status symbols available.

tions to have a bedroom for each of them. In her previous quarters, her son had slept on the living room sofa and she had wanted to continue this practice since she could not afford to furnish another room. However, although she had to take the additional bedroom, it remained empty and was used as a playroom. Meanwhile, her son still slept on the sofa and Mrs. Queene continued to protest that she was having to pay rent for a room that she did not need and could not afford to furnish.

The acquisition of major items of furniture left many gaps beneath the surface. After paying for the major purchases, there was seldom enough left to pay for the necessary replacements of expendable items. Dishes were depleted by breakage; linens became torn and frayed; scrub brushes and mops wore out, and irons needed repair. This was the time for borrowing— and for doing without.

Housekeeping Ups and Downs

Upkeep of the apartments varied from the compulsively immaculate to the unbelievably sloven. One tenant refused to have a meeting in his apartment for fear that some of the tenants might bring their children who, in turn, would soil his furniture. Some families sustained a fairly even level of housekeeping and others showed great variation. I learned a lesson from Mrs. Todd about some of these fluctuating housekeeping practices.

Mrs. Todd went from one extreme to another in her housekeeping. On one day I would almost be driven from her apartment by the acrid stench of urine, the soiled clothes scattered over the floor, and the dishes that had been standing in the sink for so long that food remnants had dried hard on them. On another day, I would find her house in apple-pie order after she had just been on a cleaning binge. Generally, the condition of her apartment would be somewhere between these two extremes.

I soon discovered that Mrs. Todd's housekeeping skills and experience were excellent and versatile, and she liked to work. She would often volunteer to help Helen and me with something we were doing, and during the course of it, criticize our performance, and insist upon doing it better. A person for whom Mrs. Todd had done some ironing said that she had never seen anyone iron clothes so well and so quickly.

I observed Mrs. Todd's inconsistent housekeeping pattern for 15 months and, gradually, its fluctuating nature began to make some sense: her housekeeping was related to her mental state! If she felt good about something, she cleaned; if she was depressed, she didn't. Most often, whether she was feeling good was dependent on her financial situation. Her spirit would noticeably perk up when she received her allotment check, but the effect was always short-lived. After she had paid her rent and the installment payments to the "three H's" and bought a supply of food, she was at the start of another long moneyless stretch that was to last until she received her next check. But during her brief respite from numbing money pressure, there was energy for housecleaning.

One occasion which spurred a thorough housecleaning was when she received some financial help from a social agency toward the replacement of two beds for her children after two months of negotiations. During the drawn-out discussions, she had become quite demoralized and had just about given up hope. When the grant came through, the transformation in her outlook was remarkable; she eagerly began planning and getting her house in readiness for the arrival of the second-hand beds she purchased with the money from the agency.

These experiences forced me to see how demoralizing want can be and how it can undermine incentive. Mrs. Todd's negligence in housekeeping could not be attributed to any lack of housekeeping skills; more valid and useful explanations would be related to low morale and the lack of incentives. It was clear that the solution to the housekeeping problems of Mrs. Todd, and others perhaps, could be found more readily in dealing with reality or situational factors, such as her lack of money and the prolonged absence of her husband, than, for example, in providing classes in homemaking.

Housekeeping choices for mothers in straitened circumstances may be sharply reduced, just as their housing choices are. The motivations and preferences related to the housekeeping behavior of some mothers in some situations are probably too quickly misunderstood, and the mothers are too frequently labeled.

For example, take the matter of insects—roaches and the like. An example of a libelous remark directed at many of the parents I knew is the following:"Well, one thing is certain, roaches do not come unless they are extended an invitation." In my experience, and in the experience of many mothers I have known, whether or not one has insects—roaches, water bugs, and the like—frequently has nothing to do with whether one keeps one's own house or apartment clean. And low-income mothers are no exception.

When I was confronted with the problem of dealing with an incursion of roaches, insecticides became a regular item on my weekly grocery list. I could not help but wonder how many of my friends and neighbors could afford to buy insecticide whenever it was needed. For many families, the hard choice was, at times, between buying insecticide or buying food. I am certain that many parents did just as Mrs. Todd did on many occasions when she needed insecticides. She went without.

III

THREE FRIENDS: BACKGROUND AND MARRIAGES

Their Family Backgrounds

The three mothers whom I came to know the best were Mrs. Todd, Mrs. Martin and Mrs. Queene. Learning about their family backgrounds and meeting some of the members of their families threw some light on what they were like and why, and it provided some clues as to what they wanted out of life, how they saw their chances, and their responses to their perceptions. My interest in knowing more about their backgrounds was stimulated by close observations of aspects of their child-rearing behavior.

There was, for example, the impassivity of Mrs. Todd, and the sharp contrast between what she said and what she did. There was Mrs. Queene's petulant harping about her marriage, and her involving her children in her marital problems. And there was Mrs. Martin's frequent and lightning transformation from the harsh to the gentle. The variability and unevenness of the child-rearing behavior of these mothers made me wonder in what ways family background had affected their chances, and, possibly as a consequence of these effects, what their children's chances were likely to be.

These three mothers had several things in common. All were natives of Washington and were in their early twenties. Their educational backgrounds were somewhat similar; one had completed the tenth; another, the eleventh; and the third, the twelfth grade. Each had been pregnant at the time of her marriage, and each had two or more preschool children.

All three mothers were from families in which there were several children: one was the oldest of seven; another, the oldest of six; and the third, the middle child of five. The parents of each mother lived with teen-age sons and daughters still in their homes. Both parents of each woman had been employed for many years mainly in Civil Service service occupations. At least two of the six working parents had achieved supervisory status in their jobs.

The parents of these three mothers are now all home owners in higher-status neighborhoods than those in which their daughters were brought up or in which they now lived.

As these women talked about their parents, they expressed the opinion that the acquisition of a car, a home and new furniture had been of paramount importance to their parents. They considered themselves casualties, in part at least, of their parents' consumption tastes and status wants.

One of these mothers said that she didn't think her family should have sacrificed her for a car. Another mother said that her family should not have sacrificed her for a house. As the women saw it, being "sacrificed," meant doing without adequate food and clothing and being pressed into substitute mother roles with younger brothers and sisters while their mother worked.

None of these three women indicated that she had a really close relationship with her mother, and each felt some resentment that she had not fared as well as her younger brothers and sisters who now had improved chances for higher education. For example, one woman's brother was a college sophomore, evidence of the improved opportunities open to the younger children of the family.

The intensity of the feelings of these mothers about their parents' "sacrificing" them is suggested in the following comments:

Mrs. Queene:
Many times we were without food for one or two days. If the car payment was due, that came first, and we just did without food even if it was two days.

Mrs. Martin:
I don't care what nobody says. A woman just can't raise children by herself. Something generally goes wrong when there is just one parent. I had both parents, but my mother always worked. My father was the one who did the raising as he could be in and out of the house all the time on his job. It just goes to show you that one parent can't do it. Look what happened. I had one sister pregnant at 16 and always truanting from school.

Mrs. Todd:
My father had two jobs and my mother had one; after school I used to keep them [younger brothers and sisters]. And sometimes in the evening I used to keep them when my mother would go out. . . . So it was just like I was the mother. I've been a mother since I was 12. . . . All my sisters and brothers depended on me a

whole lot, rather than on my mother and father. I don't think the older children should be made to feel the younger children are their responsibility. I know they should help out, but not take over the full job. It's the mother's and father's children and not the older child's.

It is indeed ironic if the parents of these wives, in their striving to "get ahead," and to acquire the visible signs of better living, including a better neighborhood in which to bring up their children, have unwittingly sacrificed a child, or children, in the process.

It appears that the struggle of some low-income families to "better themselves", by moving out of the old environs, for example, is long, hard and very costly in human and economic terms. A move to a better neighborhood may not come until some of their children are grown and out of the home. In fact, the exit (via "push" or "pull") of some of the children from the home may be the condition for some low-income parents being able to afford such a move. Thus whatever stimulus the changed environment and presumably changed status could provide is frequently lost on some, if not all, of the children.

To a certain extent, some of the young mothers in the housing project struck me as forgotten children. Their parents responded in times of trouble and crisis but there seemed to be no deep and sustained emotional ties. Mrs. Martin's parents were critical of her for having an illegitimate child. Yet, by staying at home with her own children, Mrs. Martin was consciously trying to give them some of the warmth and contact she felt she had missed because her own mother worked. Mrs. Queene's father, who had never forgiven his son-in-law for getting his daughter pregnant, had been a stern and domineering family head, even treating his wife as one of the children. But Mrs. Queene was struggling, with little success, to develop the kind of "togetherness" in her family that she did not have in her home as a child. Mrs. Todd, whose parents appeared to be so tightly budgeted in their well-furnished new home that they limited hospitality even to family members, could, in contrast, take in a child from an evicted family of six and share her scarce food supplies for several days.

These were not uncomplicated families—the project mothers' nor their parents'. They were very knowing families. In much of their behavior and their expressed standards, they straddled the deprivation and poverty from which they came and middle-class strivings and affluence. They knew the meaning of an empty refrigerator as well as a champagne fountain at a New Year's Eve party. While beds from Goodwill might be a current necessity, this did not preclude the hope that the French Provincial living room suite would some day be a reality. The child for whom there now was no money for a birthday party might someday be glamorously outfitted for a debutante's ball. They had seen it happen in their families.

Some of the young mothers in the housing project were superficially about where their parents had been twenty years before. While they may have to, or seek to, travel the same laborious path as their parents, there is a real question, for reasons that do not necessarily have anything to do with them, whether their chances and their children's chances are as good as their parents'.

Their Health Problems and Attitudes

Despite the youth of these three mothers, all had already suffered health problems. Mrs. Queene, who described herself as always having been "sickly and puny," had been hospitalized for tuberculosis for a year and a half during childhood. More recently, she had had an operation for gallstones and an appendectomy. During my stay at the project, she was hospitalized for a few days because of the pressure of a tumor on her womb while she was pregnant. There seemed to be a likelihood that she could lose the baby unless she stayed off her feet as much as possible, but she found this recommendation difficult to carry out because of her responsibilities in the home.

Mrs. Todd had had a thyroidectomy a few years ago and thought that the slight protrusion of her eyes resulted from her failure to attend the clinic for follow-up treatment; she could not make adequate plans for the care of her four children during the lengthy trips back and forth to the hospital. Her numerous physical complaints included a weight increase which she said was connected with her glandular condition. She finally returned to the clinic while I was her neighbor, and a series of tests resulted in the recommendation that she enter the hospital for a period of observation. Again she was faced with the problem of making some plan for her children and she attempted to do this by sending them to visit relatives in the South, hopefully for the summer. However, their stay was brief and the children returned home before Mrs. Todd could be admitted to the hospital. It was not until more than a year later, after her husband returned from his tour of duty, that she finally did enter the hospital.

At age 13, Mrs. Martin had been hospitalized for polio. Discharged in a wheel chair after a two-and-a-half-year hospital stay, she had made a valiant nine-year struggle to walk without crutches or braces. When I commented on the success she seemed to have made, her response was, "Do you want me to tell you the truth? I feel very slighted. I don't see why I had to be the one to get it." She attributed her determination to overcome her handicap to the fact that she did not like to ask people for help and did not like people to try to do things for her. Her second health problem was a liver ailment. Sporadic in her clinic attendance, she complained of the cost of prescriptions. One prescription had cost $4.95 at the city hospital, and this was more than she could afford to pay.

Of the three mothers, Mrs. Queene was perhaps the most conscientious about getting medical care. She was proud of giving birth to her children in a private hospital and had made early arrangements for her third delivery. Her attendance at a prenatal clinic was regular and she looked forward to her hospitalization as a pleasurable experience. Mrs. Martin, on the other hand, avoided prenatal clinics, preferring to wait until the last minute for hospitalization. Part of her reluctance was connected with her embarrassment over vaginal examinations.

The two major problems which these mothers had with respect to obtaining medical care was in making adequate arrangements for their children while they attended clinics and in making provisions for the maintenance of their homes during hospitalizations. They called upon relatives and neighbors and received some kind of help from them on occasion, but there was always an element of insecurity to these plans; a plan could be made for one week, but perhaps not for the next. Thus, the mothers tended to neglect their own health, a practice which had a decided effect on the child care had provided since a half-sick mother just cannot perform as well as a healthy one.

Although rest had also been prescribed for Mrs. Todd, she felt that she never got any. After she had yielded to the plea of one of her sisters to take care of her nephew for a few days, she remarked rather ruefully, "She's talking about giving her a rest, but who's going to give me a rest?"

Their Marriages

In the housing project population, there were marriages that were stable and unstable, violent and nonviolent, loving and unloving, male-dominated and female-dominated. Any kind you could name was likely to be there. It was not unusual to see an open demonstration of affection between husband and wife, nor was it exceptional to hear a torrent of epithets float from an open window as an angry wife chastened her errant husband on his return after midnight. It was sobering to learn that a husband had murdered his estranged wife, a tenant with whom I had been friendly. It was saddening to see a husband return from service to find himself unwanted, his place usurped. And it was thought-provoking to hear more than one young woman say that if she ever got out of this marriage, she did not want another. But somehow the mixture of domestic joy and bitterness, hope and desperation, seemed to make sense, given the imperatives of economic insecurity and living, in a public-housing project.

Mrs. Harris, the dowager queen of the court, had much to say on the subject of marriage. To her, marriage was more than a love affair; it was also a business affair. "Do what you say you're going to do and be responsible for your family." Marrying at age 32, she had had three children and 38 years of a happy married life before she was widowed. Her "good husband" had a "good job" and "took care of his family". The social-security benefits on which she now lived were a testimony to this. None of my three young friends was as positive as Mrs. Harris about her marriage.

Mrs. Todd: When I first moved into the project, Mrs. Todd talked constantly of her husband, counting the days until his return from overseas and wondering how she was going to make it with her four children until then. Every night she wrote long letters to him, and, almost daily, she received similar ones from him.

On one occasion when Mrs. Todd visited us, Helen was practicing her diction on the tape recorder and soon we were all involved. Excusing herself, Mrs. Todd went home, returning with a text book from which she gave a passionate rendition of an excerpt from James Weldon Johnson's "God's Trombones." I chose Elizabeth Barrett Browning's sonnet which begins, "How do I love thee? Let me count the ways." Impressed with the sentiment of the sonnet, Mrs. Todd immediately copied it to send to her husband. Two days later she greeted me with, "Guess what? I had a letter from my husband today and he wrote me the last lines of that same poem I sent him!"

. . . I love thee with the breath, smiles, tears, of all my life! and, if God choose, I shall but love thee better after death.

Mrs. Todd had known her husband since she was 12 years old. He had been her one close friend. It was to his home that she would sometimes go when she was hungry, and his mother would give her food. She and her husband had developed a kind of "real understanding" that most people just did not comprehend; they could tell each other whatever was on their minds. However, she was not too sure but that their love was more the "brother-sister kind" than the "man and woman kind."

At one point, she described herself as being more like the maid in the family, keeping the house and the clothes clean and preparing the meals while her husband took charge of the children. During her husband's absence, she began to question whether she wanted her marriage to continue in this way and spoke about how the problem of being a woman can sometimes "boil up" in her:

> The woman has to be responsible for pleasing everybody, the husband and the children. She should do everything in her power to please her husband and not make him feel like he's helpless all the time. Something comes up and I don't want to do it—well, I do it anyway because I know it would be pleasing everybody else. But I don't think I should please a lot of people and displease myself. In the future I won't be doing so much to try to please as I did before because sometimes it all boils up in me. I just think from now on I'll try to do my best but I won't overdo it. I think that in the past I overdid it trying to be a good wife and a good mother and I was taken for granted about everything.

Despite these concerns about the proper parts for wives and husbands, Mrs. Todd was unwilling to listen to the denunciations of her neighbor, Mrs. Norris, "who just seemed to hate men and was always saying that men were dogs and no good." The neighbor criticized Mrs. Todd for not agreeing with her that children come first. Mrs. Todd said she had no reason for hating men because she and her husband had always gotten along all right. During a taped interview on what she considered the most important thing to a woman, Mrs. Todd pondered her priorities and described the complicated, sometimes competitive, demands of husbands and children:

> I'd say the most important thing would be my husband. If you go all through life and everything is your children, your children, your children, and you never think about doing this for your husband or trying to make things better here or trying to make things better there, you are neglectful of your husband.

He's probably only staying there until the children are out of the way because they were his responsibility and he was a good father and a husband. By that time the children are gone and you are so worked up in doing things for the children that you forgot about your husband.

Therefore, I would say that my husband comes first because my children would grow up and leave me and lead lives of their own. And, although I wouldn't nelect my children, I still say my husband would come first.

Mrs. Martin: The matter of who comes first, the husband or the children, was uncomplicated for Mrs. Martin; her experience had taught her that "you just can't put no trust in a man".

The most important thing to me is my children. Other things come after them. Maybe that's why I'm not married now. A man comes in second. He's still lucky he comes in second as I'm the one that comes in last!

She arrived at this position on the basis of a marriage that had lasted about three years. Mrs. Martin described her husband as "no good" because he did not pay his bills, particularly the rent. As a result, they were constantly on the move and threatened with eviction. After one eviction, their children had to be placed temporarily in Junior Village, a Washington, D.C., institution for the temporary care of dependent children.

In addition to charging her husband with failure to take care of his family financially, Mrs. Martin complained that he ran around with other women. Mrs. Martin's father had advised her that it was natural for men to run awhile before they settled down. She had tried to adjust to this behavior, but the problems of financial support continued to be acute even though her husband was regularly employed. Tiring of his behavior, Mrs. Martin told her husband that if he could not take care of his family, he should leave. She permitted him to remain until he found a place to live, then helped him pack.

Since their separation, there had been continual problems around nonsupport; Mrs. Martin complained about what she considered court laxity in enforcing the support order. She believed that court laxity encouraged her husband to think that he could get away with almost anything. He appeared unworried about her threats to return to court, and taunted her about legal help he could get through "his connections" at work. She thought that her husband had the knack of making his story more believable to the court than she could make hers. She cited the fact that he had succeeded in getting a $5 reduction in the court order although she was quite sure that he was concealing information about the tips he made on his job.

After their separation, Mr. Martin made one attempt at reconciliation. However, Mrs. Martin heard nothing more from him after she told him that he could come back provided that he turned over his paycheck so that she could pay the bills. She was interested in obtaining a divorce if she did not have to pay for it: "If he wants it, he can get it and pay for it. He has wasted enough money already to pay for one."

She doubted whether she would ever get married again as she just didn't have confidence in men any more.

Mrs. Queene: Mrs. Queene's marriage had a more adequate financial base than that of the other two mothers. This was partly due to the fact that she had only two children; each of the other mothers had four. Her husband's weekly $75 pay check also helped ease matters; the moneyless stretches for her family were not as long as they were for the families of the other two mothers.

Mrs. Queene also had problems. She thought that her husband "ran around" too much and did not spend enough time with his family. There had been two separations, the first when Mrs. Queene was six months pregnant with her first child, and the second when her second child was one month old. During my stay in the project, she talked constantly of leaving her husband again.

Mrs. Martin ridiculed Mrs. Queene's attitude, insisting that as long as Mr. Queene took care of his family as he did, Mrs. Queene should not worry since "most men run until they are about 30 and then they settle down". A comparable attitude was implied by Mrs. Todd when she recounted a friend's similar suspicions about her husband. Mrs. Todd concluded, "But he does treat her nice, though. You should see the nice bedroom suite he bought her."

The statements of these mothers seemed to suggest that if a wife has to compromise her position about marital fidelity, adequate support is a prerequisite.

Mrs. Queene, however, was not ready to make this compromise. She could not accept her husband's thinking that as long as he paid the rent and bought the food, she should have nothing to say about their relationship. She wanted more than that and told him: "You have to give yourself. If you really love somebody, love shows in what you do." She did not want to be "second choice to nobody" and wanted to be loved "just like he does".

Having witnessed violent arguments and fights between her parents, Mrs. Queene wanted a different kind of marriage for herself but knew that just the absence of fighting was not enough. Expressing her disappointment, hurt, and bitterness, she said:

Maybe I should be different. When he comes home, I don't start throwing things at him like some people would do. But he thinks it's something because he don't come home and fight on me like some men do. I have to give him credit for that, but he still doesn't seem to know what marriage should be like. I guess it's the way he was brought up.

That man has hurt me so bad. I thought that marriage was love and trust, but I guess that I am wrong. When I go out I always tell him where I'm going but I never know where he is going. The way I feel about him is that I don't think I would give him a glass of water if he was sick and down. He thinks more of his friends and pleasures than he does of me and the children.

Mrs. Queene also expressed her thoughts about who comes first in her family. She revealed her priorities had been affected by her husband's behavior:

> I have always told him my children come first. When I didn't even have [my first child] he was running around then. He would come home any hour of the night and ask me to get up and fix a meal for him. I would always do whatever he said, but I finally got wise to myself.

> Now he says that I am not the girl that I used to be. Sure I've changed! I changed after the first time I left him and it was because of the way he was running around.*

Mrs. Queene's struggle over what to do in her situation was a monumental one. On the one hand, she wanted to leave because, "if I'm living with him and I've still got to be a mother and a father, then I don't need him." On the other hand, she had serious misgivings about a separation, mainly related to the well-being of the children:

> . . . mostly for the children's sake and mine, I wish we could make it. I really don't want to separate. After all, you read about all this delinquency and in most cases, it is because the man is gone and the mother is at work and the children are on their own. That's what happens, and I don't want it to happen to my children.

Their Husbands

In the three families under discussion the only husband whom I knew was Mr. Queene and my contact with him was brief and passing. However, the wives' discussions

---

* This is probably closer to a rather universal reaction of women with philandering husbands than to engrained female hostility or to aspects of a matriarchal tradition.

yielded their images of their husbands. As they discussed their husbands, they echoed attitudes that I was getting in my observations and interviews with families outside the public housing project.

Mr. Queene: A personable, outgoing man in his late twenties, Mr. Queene always gave me a pleasant greeting when I saw him in his mechanics' overalls on his way to and from work. He was from a large family in a nearby state. His mother was reputed to be a heavy drinker, who, in fits of anger, would throw pots and pans at her children. His father introduced Mr. Queene to tavern life at an early age and before Mr. Queene was 14, he saw his father killed in a tavern brawl. They had been bystanders and his father was struck and killed by an iron bar that someone had thrown. Soon afterwards, Mr. Queene ran away from home and never returned there to live.

Mr. Queene had less than a fifth-grade education as compared to his wife's tenth-grade education. According to his wife, he was nearly illiterate but could read and write a little. He talked about going back to night school, but he had never done so. One of the reasons they had a telephone was to allow him to call her and ask her how to spell the words he needed to use in making out bills for mechanical repairs. At times she believed that the only reason he held on to their marriage was that he needed her help in these matters. She had tried to tell him that his lack of education was nothing to be ashamed of since a person who did well despite little formal education was sometimes complimented for overcoming this handicap. Mr. Queene did hold his job and seemed to be well thought of by his employer.

Mrs. Queene thought that her husband tried to cover up his lack of education with "big talk". He did not want his friends to know that he had no education. He was constantly telling people tales about things he had done and places he had been. He could tell convincing stories about the bid he had made on a parking lot or the candy store he planned to buy. Sometimes he talked of going back to work for a bootlegger he once worked for, because then he used to have hundreds of dollars in his pocket. Not knowing what to believe, Mrs. Queene could only show annoyance at these fantasies.*

Mr. Queene's desire for a car helped precipitate a marital crisis in which the control of money was an issue. His wife had not wanted the car and refused to join him in signing a note for it, but he had been able to get a bank loan anyway. When he purchased the car, he took the management of money away from his wife, and periodically he neglected to give her the $20 a week he had decided was the allotment to run the household. According to Mrs. Queene, the $55 monthly used-car bill would not have been too great a strain if he had managed the money properly, since their other bills were small.

The increased mobility Mr. Queene achieved with the car kept him away from home more and more. Before he bought the car, he had spent much more time around the house. He used to take the children out for walks to the playground and, in general, did more things with his family. But with the car, said his wife, "He goes out, runs around, and messes up on money." An added problem was his occasional drinking. Mrs. Queene was in constant fear that he might have an accident while under the influence of alcohol, and as a result lose the driver's license which he needed on his job.

Mr. Todd: Like Mr. Queene, Mr. Todd had his fantasies too, but he expressed them differently. He confided his frustration in letters to his wife, for example:

I do love you and always will, so if I seem hard at times it's because I'm hurt inside . . . . I dream about being things I could never be, but it would be a lot of fun trying to do things.

Limited civilian choices made Mr. Todd a captive of the armed services. He had enlisted several years earlier when his education was abruptly interrupted by his wife's preg-

* She expressed much less compassion, for example, than a mother who, in trying to explain why men seem to drink so much, said, "They all wants things they cannot get."

nancy and their marriage. A high-school graduate, he gave up an athletic scholarship awarded by a Negro college because he had to support his family. He doubted that he could find a civilian job; he had already tried and failed.

After one period of enlistment, he came out of the service and looked desperately for work, with no immediate success. He took various civil service examinations. No immediate results were forthcoming. Finally he managed to get hired at the Post Office during the Christmas rush, only to have his last paycheck stolen from his mailbox. With no money and no job, he saw no alternative but to re-enlist.

Bitter about his failure to get promotions as fast as white servicemen got them, he vented some of his feelings in his letters to his wife. He had not had a promotion in three years although he had ability in the clerical capacity in which he worked. Even the recommendations of his commanding officers were to no avail.

Describing how fed up he was, he wrote to his wife that he was made to feel that he didn't count for anything; it was only when he asked for leave that he suddenly became indispensable. He spoke of writing to Headquarters about the situation, knowing that he might get in trouble, but feeling that someone had to speak up. Perhaps whatever he said might help someone else later on, even though it might not help him.

On the surface, Mrs. Todd seemed unmoved by this situation. When I asked her what she thought about the experiences her husband was having, she said, "I'm going to tell him like he tells me: 'Keep your petty troubles to yourself!' " I did not fully understand the significance of this statement when Mrs. Todd first made it, and it seemed to me a rather heartless thing to say. But, as I came to know her better and to know what her "troubles" were, it seemed to me that what she was doing was declaring the limits of her tolerance. Her own situation was more than enough to bear without hearing her husband's problems.

Mr. Todd's mother, whom I met, was a warm, motherly widow in her seventies. Mr. Todd was the seventh of her children, and there was an 18-year gap between Mr. Todd and next older child. She maintained a regular contact with her daughter-in-law and grandchildren and showed interest in many ways; for example, by trying to help out the family during her son's absence. Still doing an occasional day's work a week for a family for whom she had worked for years, she would sometimes buy food and clothing for her grandchildren out of her scant income.

Mr. Martin: The husband about whom I knew least was Mr. Martin, but there were a few clues to his behavior and general characteristics. Mrs. Martin told me that her husband was the only boy in his family and that, as far as she was concerned, this was as bad as being an only child. Implying that he had been "spoiled", she said that his mother would occasionally bail him out of financial difficulty by paying the rent for their family, even though her son was employed. Mrs. Martin suggested that this encouraged irresponsibility in her husband, particularly when it came to supporting his family.

After the separation from his wife, Mr. Martin began going with a woman who was older than he and, on one occasion, had asked for a divorce so that he could marry her. Mrs. Martin said she disapproved of the woman because she was older than Mr. Martin and because the woman had the reputation of being a heavy drinker. She refused her husband's request for a divorce: "If he thinks I'm going to let a woman like that be my children's stepmother and thinks that he is going to take them and have them visit her, he's crazy!"

To some extent, Mr. Martin still kept tabs on his wife and her whereabouts. According to her, he generally had his facts right when he would tell her about some place he knew she had been. On one occasion, she was indignant at his criticism of her for having been at a party when she "should have been at home taking care of his children." Her assessment of Mr. Martin, as well as another clue as to what she wanted in a husband, was suggested one day when she shifted from a discussion of him to talk about a man she knew that she always saw loafing on a street corner. When she asked this man why he didn't work, he told her that he picks up numbers for a few hours each day. Then she said to me perplexedly, "Why is it that men just don't seem to work any more? All they do is pick up a few numbers and that is all."

Mrs. Martin's boyfriend: The man I first thought was Mr. Martin turned out to be Mrs. Martin's boyfriend, Mr. Tompkins, the father of her last child. I had seen him on a few occasions with her and her children, and he had always appeared quite solicitous of their welfare. I eventually expressed my confusion to Mrs. Martin. Nodding toward the baby in her lap, she clarified the situation for me. Her remarks provided an unmistakable comparison of the two men. "This is not my husband's baby," she said. "This baby's father takes care of her!"

Mr. Tompkins never missed bringing his weekly contribution for his daughter's support; he kept her well clothed and frequently took her to his home on weekends. The contrast between her husband's and her boyfriend's patterns of support of the children they had fathered probably made it easier for Mrs. Martin to tell me that she was not ashamed of her baby born out of wedlock; she said repeatedly that she liked and respected the baby's father.

Mr. Tompkins, the baby's father, was single, a husky six-footer about 28 years old, quiet and reserved. He was the oldest of four children, the only boy. His father had died when his mother was pregnant with the youngest child, who was about eight years younger than Mr. Tompkins. When he was in the ninth grade, he dropped out of school in order to help his mother who did domestic work. According to Mrs. Martin, "His mother is 45 but looks like 60; when she dies, it will be from weariness." Mr. Tompkins was regularly employed as a truck driver and was buying the air-conditioned home in which he lived with his mother and sisters.

Mrs. Martin said that Mrs. Tompkins thought the sun rose and set on her son and waited on him "hand and foot". Mr. Tompkins spent much of his time at home with his mother and did not "run around". Jealous of his mother's suitors, he once knocked Mrs. Martin down when she teased him about his mother's having a boyfriend, exclaiming, "My mother's not no good like you!" Mrs. Martin thought that, in a way, she and Mr. Tompkins were alike since they both distrusted the opposite sex.

Mr. Tompkins had asked Mrs. Martin to marry him and she had refused. Intermittently, he renewed the offer of marriage. Mrs. Martin had several reasons for being uninterested in marriage at that stage in her life. Apparently, she and Mr. Tompkins had lived together for a short period; Mrs. Martin said she had put him out when she found he expected her to wait on him as his mother did. She also found him too grouchy; she had had enough fussing with her husband and did not want any more. She was afraid that "if he got that piece of paper on me", he would feel that he could "hit on [her] like he hits on his younger sisters". Another of her fears was related to the fact that she thought Mr. Tompkins had changed since the birth of their daughter; that is, that he gave most of his affection to his child and very little to her and the other children. She anticipated conflict over child-rearing methods because she did not like the way he was spoiling the baby who could already "wrap him around her finger". Like a number of low-income mothers outside the project, Mrs. Martin seemed particularly fearful of the unknowns, as well as the knowns, involved in taking on a stepfather for her children. She said that she sometimes thought she might get married, but it would not be until the children were in junior high school.

An Overview of Marriage

The concerns of these mothers about marriage and the family were recurrent in and outside the housing project. They related to the qualities of the "good man" and the "no good man", the meaning and importance of love and fidelity in marriage, and the critical importance of support and nonsupport to mothers and children.

The vulnerability of these marriages was crucially associated with job insecurity, nonsupport, and extramarital relationships.* A critical factor was the pressure and strain

---

* To add "and vice versa" would probably not be amiss. But to pursue this aspect of marital relations among the poor requires more space and time, if not data, than are now at my disposal.

placed on the husband who could not meet the wife's basic demand for adequate financial support. The efforts of some husbands to ease the pressure, to seek escape from the classic dilemma of the economically inadequate father, were understood better after I had observed the family situations of my friends over a considerable period of time.

The mothers' comments bore signs of influences and recollections of their early lives that carried over into their marriages. Mrs. Todd, who had cared for her younger sisters and brothers since she was 12, commented, "All my life I felt like I was married, but I just didn't have no husband." This thought, expressed in a number of ways by other mothers, suggests one reason why Mrs. Todd said her husband comes first: having a husband was the new element in her life—not having to bring up children. A male counterpart of Mrs. Todd in some ways was Mr. Tompkins who had, in effect, played a father and husband role in his own fatherless family. It is easy to speculate on the relationship between his fulfilling this dual responsibility with his younger siblings and widowed mother, and the fact that he has not married.

Mrs. Queene appeared to have very little affection to give her husband; however, she tried to avoid in her marriage the violence she had witnessed in her parents' relationship. She was also trying to prevent having any of her children "sacrificed" for a car as she thought she had been sacrificed.

Mrs. Martin was critical of her mother and spoke of her "failure" as a parent, viewing her mother's employment as the chief cause of her child-rearing problems. She steadfastly repeated: "Every mother should stay home with her children."

Some of the younger mothers wanted to add some of the ingredients that they remembered as missing from their childhood family experiences to their own marriages; however, they often seemed unskilled and inexperienced in what to do and how to do it. Sometimes they acknowledged their limitations. Smarting from the deprivations that they associated with their parents' efforts to purchase homes, none of these three young women talked of home ownership for herself. A partial reason might have been that it was too early in their lives for them to do so. They did, however, give some clues as to where they would like to be going. Mrs. Todd outlined her preferred future:

> I guess when you ask someone what they want out of life, they would say the same things, probably a house, health and maybe a car or something like that. But I don't think having a house or a car are more important than having yourself, your husband and your children together and happy. And I think that the most I would want out of life would be just to have a home together, my children together and me and my husband together. And if along the way we would get a house and a car—well, that would be okay too, but I think the other things comes first. . . . I think that in my case it would be just having a nice home and health and happiness more than anything else.

The Poverty of Sex

Mrs. Queene criticized her husband because he did not "give himself" to his marriage; he, in turn, accused her of being undemonstrative. He told her that she had no idea how happy it would make him if she met him at the door with a kiss when he came home from work. Her response was: "That's the way I am and that's that."

There was plenty of evidence that she actually had more concern than her quick, probably defensive, retort suggests. From time to time, she would resolve to try to behave differently. She would plan how she would act when her husband came home, but, when he arrived on the scene, she just couldn't carry off her plan. She said that she had read articles about women who were frigid and thought that perhaps she might be like that. Describing their marital relationship, she said:

> I'm not as affectionate as he is. I just can't be affectionate. I was never affectionate as a child. He likes to kiss a lot but I get tired of it. My grandmother is the

only one in the family who does a lot of hugging and kissing, but no one else in my family does.

The unresponsiveness that Mrs. Queene described was also expressed by the other two mothers. On one occasion, Mrs. Todd said, "I can't get enthused about anything, nothing bothers me." On another occasion, while musing, she said that she didn't know why she loved her husband so much because he didn't give her any money and she was not interested in sex. She said, "It's the same with my husband—he's just not too interested." She thought of sex more as an obligation than a pleasure and their love was more the "brother-sister kind".*

Mrs. Todd was five months pregnant before she knew she was pregnant, and she said she would not have known it then had her father not told her.

Like many of the mothers observed by the Child Rearing Study, Mrs. Martin's discovery of sex was traumatic and much of her subsequent experience with it distasteful. Her mother had told her nothing about sex, and her father only contributed the warning: "All a man wants is what's between your legs; all they want is to give you a baby." In her description of her first sex experience, Mrs. Martin graphically described her motivation for entering the act, the mixture of hurt and fear, and the anticlimactic aftermath:

All my girl friends had already done it and kept talking about it and teasing me because I hadn't. So I decided that one day when Howard came over, I would do something about it. When he came over, I took him to the playground. I am sure sorry I did because it wasn't

* In many ways their situation reminded me of a description another young mother had given of the factors she thought gave rise to premarital pregnancy. She said: "I think it stems from working parents, lack of interest and love from parents, broken homes. I feel that the son or daughter finds in someone else something that is missing from home. A girl finds a boy who is being treated the same way she is being treated at home. They say: 'They don't like us anymore. I don't get along at home.' 'Well I don't either. Let's get together,' but they try to console one another, and out of that comes a great big problem!"

nothing like I expected. Oh, it hurt me so much. I was trying to scream and he kept his hand over my mouth. I was so mad with him when I got up that I wouldn't even let him walk beside me. I walked in front and he walked behind me. I stopped by a girlfriend's house and told her and her mother about it. Her mother was surprised that I did not know anything and she sat down and told me what it was all about. I had never heard anything about a cherry before that time. Mama and Daddy just never spoke to us about things like that.

Part of the reason Mrs. Martin was not too anxious to marry Mr. Tomkins was that he was "hot natured", and she was not too interested in sex. She reported that they had gone together a year before having sexual relations and, even then, she could have done without it. She thought that all men were "hot in the hindparts". She also thought that, even if you were married, sexual intercourse once every three weeks was enough.

Mrs. Martin described her conflict:

Take me, for instance. I might have a desire for a man once in three months and I don't see any reason why I shouldn't go ahead and have one. But, you know, I still think it's nasty.* I always feel so ashamed when it is all over. As far as I'm concerned, I could do without it.

Some of the attitudes of Mrs. Harris, who was in her seventies, about marital sex and the part the wife should play contrasted sharply with those of the young mothers. She attributed part of the success of her marriage to the fact that she always met her husband's wishes with regard to sexual intercourse; she believed that she could truthfully say that her husband had never had another woman during their marriage. She was critical of women who refused to

---

* The description of sex as "nasty" is strikingly recurrent in CRS materials.

meet the sexual demands of their husbands. She advised one woman who was complaining of her husband's late hours, "If you sew your stuff up, you can't expect anything else because while you do that there is always someone out there who is willing to open up."

Mrs. Harris added:

The trouble with men is that they are like animals. They wants everything they can get. They don't know what they wants or who they wants, but they wants it when they wants it.*

One day while visiting Mrs. Martin, I had an opportunity to explore further this theme about man's "animal nature" with respect to sex. Marie, an outspoken woman about age 30, was present. During our conversation, she and Mrs. Martin constantly referred to men as dirty dogs. When I asked the reason for this characterization, Marie volunteered the following: when she was 15 years old, she had gone on a domestic job to the home of a white woman. After showing Marie what she wanted done, the woman left the house. Her husband remained at home while Marie went about her work. Part of the time he was playing cards with some male friends who eventually left. When Marie finished her work, the man asked her if she wanted a dollar. Marie told him that she wanted the money she had earned. He then pushed her down on a bed, exposed himself, and grabbed her. Relaxing enough to throw him off guard, Marie suddenly reached for an iron she had seen on the mantel over the bed and "came down on his face with it". Blood gushed from his face as she ran screaming from the apartment. Hearing Marie's screams, a woman in the building came to the rescue and called the police who took Marie, still hysterical, back to the apartment. They found the man just as she had described him and, according to Marie, "lit into the man and gave him a good working over".

* References to the "animal nature" of men were recurrent among women interviewed and observed for CRS.

Marie's mother pressed charges, and the man was jailed. His wife came to their home pleading for her husband, and Marie could not understand what the woman would want with her husband after knowing what he had done. Marie's mother decided that since Marie had not been raped and had actually injured him with the iron, the man had already gotten the punishment he deserved. She heeded his wife's pleas and dropped the charges.

Finishing the description of this incident and commenting on her behavior, Marie said that she had fought fiercely since, "After all, I was a virgin and I was fighting for my honor."

The second experience Marie recounted involved her stepfather. He made advances to Marie and she was reluctant to tell her mother who was ill at the time, for fear of upsetting her. Instead, she threatened her stepfather with exposure if he ever repeated his advances; he never did. She said that she had never told anyone about this incident until recently, when her sister made a comment about what a nice person their stepfather was. At this point, Mrs. Martin related her story: about two years ago, Mrs. Martin was raped by a friend's husband. Her friend had gone out of town and had asked Mrs. Martin to keep her mail for her. Her friend's husband came to Mrs. Martin's home to get the mail and forced himself on her. Mrs. Martin called her father and brother who had the man arrested.

My observations and hearing at first hand such accounts as the above sharpened my awareness about the lack of accurate knowledge about, and the need for better understanding of, the sex life of lower-income groups. They coincide with field reports and observations of other CRS staff members.

During one speculative interchange about sex and poverty, the project director said:

The thing that interests me about the materials we have is the asexuality. We hear a lot of talk about the sexuality of the poor and the like. But the quality of sex we get to see or sense in much of CRS' materials strikes me as reflecting a kind of poignant non-passion, and this last seems to me to be true in many, many instances where there appears to be an aggressive, even frantic, quality to sex.

IV

THREE FRIENDS: MOTHERS AND CHILDREN

On Parental Responsibility

Bringing up children, especially small children, was not an easy matter for the mothers. Among my first, rather strong expectations, was that the inviting court would be swarming daily with children; but I was soon struck, and for a while puzzled, by the underutilization of the court.

At first I thought that the small number of children in the court was due to the brisk spring weather and the still relatively short days. However, the days grew longer and the weather grew warmer and there was still no appreciable change in the number of the children in the court. Thinking that this might be a Monday-to-Friday school day phenomenon, I then watched to see what would happen on Saturdays. But, again on Saturdays, the court was consistently empty until late afternoon. I speculated that Saturday chores took precedence and, therefore, were a major deterrent to use of the court.

On Sundays, activities in the court were at a virtual standstill; I think I correctly attributed this to the fact that many of the children were dressed in their Sunday best and were observing their parents' warnings to keep themselves clean. But I was still plagued by the feeling that there were just not enough children in the court compared to the proportion of children in the housing-project population.

Summer vacation brought no major change in the numbers of children using the court. Winter snows failed to lure sled riders. There were few snow battles in the court, and not a snowman appeared, despite a ten-inch fall.

Gradually, I began to realize that many young mothers were virtually imprisoned behind the walls of the building. Getting out of the apartment and down to the court was a major operation for many women with children of pre-school age. This was the real deterrent to a greater use of the court.

First, there was the need to try to make the trip between feeding schedules and naps. The situation was more difficult because the children could not be relied upon to time their habits appropriately. Dressing all the children to take them into the court was also time consuming.

In order to go to the store to get a forgotten loaf of bread, for example, a parent had four alternatives: she could dress the children and take them with her, get a baby sitter to stay with them, notify a neighbor to listen for any undue noises or leave the children by themselves. All four methods were used; some parents used each method on more than one occasion.

My impressions after 15 months were that the overwhelming majority of parents cared deeply about, and were concerned about, the welfare of their children. Their concern took many forms and had many dimensions. Concern about children might be focused on attempting to obtain the basic necessities of life for them or meeting all the needs of all the children. There was seldom total absence of concern about a child or children on the part of parents.*

Elders speak about child rearing. The Girls did not hesitate to express their opinions of the younger generation of mothers. What they said about the young mothers was more sad than vicious, more puzzled than envious, more simple than complex—but withal, sharp and confident. Indications that they felt themselves superior came out in various ways.

* Of course, fathers and mothers may have differed in instances as to which concerns were to be shared, which were to be exclusively those of mother and of father, as well as about the ranking of child-rearing concerns.

Some of these mothers are the ones that need to be slapped. They don't have any patience. The trouble is they have children too soon. They are not ready for them. Many a one had to come out of school because she was pregnant.

* * *

These people don't know nothing about raisin' children. Raisin' children is simple. I raised plenty of white children—and colored, too. All you got to do is be positive. Let 'em know you mean what you say.

* * *

If they aren't taught to mind at home you can't expect them to act any different here. It's not like when I was a child. If someone told you not to do something, you dasn't do it as you knew they would tell your parents and you would get a whipping.

* * *

These parents don't raise children nowadays; the children raises them!

The Girls were not unique in their thinking; the same kinds of statements came frequently from parents in their thirties and forties. Some said, "Times have changed," or, "It's not like it was when I was coming up."

Whether these expressions suggest yearnings for the good old days or whether they reflect significant changes in child-rearing settings and practices among the poor is not an issue here. They *do* show these parents' uneasiness about the present. Some of the young mothers shared this uneasiness and were critical of aspects of their own child-rearing performances.

Asked what she considered good parents to be, Mrs. Todd said:

A good mother is one who tries to lead her children right or tries to do the right thing for them in everyday life, or wasn't too cuddlesome, or wasn't too harsh with the children and tried to understand them. The father is a good provider if he does the same things I said about the mother.

But her appraisal of herself was different:

I don't think that now I'm being as good a mother as I should be. I won't say why, when, or where, but I don't think so.

And Mrs. Martin had her doubts:

Some children just got it in them to be bad. I'm looking for one or even two of mine to turn out bad. Even in the best of families you have a bad egg. But you can't down a woman for trying without a man.

Added Specifics of Child Rearing: Mrs. Todd

Four children* were more than Mrs. Todd had wanted. She would have preferred only three. There were many indications, sometimes from Mrs. Todd, that even three would have been too many. One outstanding characteristic of her child-rearing behavior was the contrast between what she said and what she did.

Needs of children, as perceived and stated. Expanding in a taped interview on what she considered the most important things a child should have, Mrs. Todd specified four needs in this order:

Children need a good understanding with their parents. What I refer to mostly right now would be teenage-adult relationships. I think they shouldn't be too close, or they shouldn't be too far apart. I think that the mother shouldn't be domineering, and that the father shouldn't be domineering. They all should try to fix things up and work things out. . . . I don't think they should be too harsh because it seems to me that if they are, it leads the children on the wrongdoing, and

* They were Elsie, age five; Philip, age four; Nicholas, age three; Shirley, age nine months.

therefore they don't have any guidance or understanding between the mother and father. I think they should do things together, take trips together, play together, and everything they do in the home they should do together.

I don't think that younger children should be petted too much or neglected too much. But I think that they should know that her mother is the mother and that they are not independent yet. They should listen to what each other says, do what they're told, I guess. . . . Petting too much is, I would say, a mother who babies the child. If he's a boy, and he falls down and hurts himself, and she's always petting him; then each time he falls, instead of getting up and brushing off, he has to run to his mother. It's also not giving in to everything he wants.

By neglecting them, I would say, it is not taking any interest in the things they want to do. When they come to you and ask certain things or questions about things, most people who are neglectful would probably say, "Go ahead and be about your business," or "I have something else to do," or, "You go and play." Neglecting them is also not caring for them in their everyday routine life, such as cleaning them up and feeding them. I think that every child should have some sort of preschool training. That means the mother should read to them and the mother should teach them and try to help them with things they bring home from school so that they would learn more in school. And I think that if she didn't, she probably would be neglectful.

Children need some kind of church life. If they start out in church, the church could contribute to them being truthful, having a lot more understanding of people and just clean everyday living, because I know. Maybe some children won't have a good life at home, and maybe when they go to a church or to something like a settlement house and get the guidance of other adults—well, then it's different. Maybe the atmosphere just wasn't as becoming [at home] as when they were in church or somewhere else.

Did church do anything for you?

To a certain extent it did. I did go to church right regular for a number of years, but I was made to go since I didn't like it. After a while it just grew on me, and I felt better there than at home or other places.

Children need decent food, clothing and shelter. I'm not saying that they should have the best of everything or the worst of everything—decent food, not just anything thrown together. I'm talking about some mothers; they have so much else to do that they just throw anything together. Sometimes, in order to go about their business, they would just give them some cookies or candy or anything just to fill them up, not caring whether it was good for them or not.

Clothing? Well, I think anything would probably be decent if it was—I don't know why I keep using the word "decent"—but anything would be good enough if it wasn't dirty. The clothing should be kept clean. And shelter? Just to have a roof over their heads if the place they are living in is not contaminated or dirty.

The mother should keep a clean house, clean for the children and whoever is living in the house. And I guess that's all I can say about what I mean about food, shelter and clothing. I wouldn't say that it would have to be extravagant, just clean and wholesome.

Children need sensible teaching by their parents, teachers, ministers and all the adults they come in contact with. I think they should teach a child to be respectful truthful, and to be well behaved and well mannered. They should teach them how to get along with other adults and other children, especially other children, and to share. If they were a church-going family, they would probably be well introduced to the church, and to school if they were out of the preschool age. By the time they were five, they would have been introduced to all those things and I think it would be beneficial to them as they grow older. They would know these things, the right and the wrong things; then there wouldn't be too much possibility that they would come out wrong at the end.

What else?

I would say sensible—or something of value to the children, not anything that wouldn't be of value to them. I think adults should go by: 'Practice what you preach.' Why should a mother or father tell a child not to go out and do certain things and they [the parents] are going out and doing it themselves—in the home too!

Like what?

Maybe they were telling a boy, 'I don't want you gambling or drinking, or doing this or that.' When he does, he gets punished, and all the while they are doing it themselves.

The relationship of some of her opinions to recollections of her own upbringing was suggested in her response to a question about whether she was bringing up her children the way she was brought up:

No, I don't think so. I think I'll try to bring them up better than my mother and father brought me up and teach them more than what was taught to me.

In what ways would you try to improve upon the way you were brought up?

Well, for one thing, I had a mother and father that

weren't strict. I think they should have been more strict than they were. We never did have an understanding between each other, and we still haven't. We never were close. We just never did have an understanding of each other. I didn't understand them and I'm afraid that they didn't seem to understand me.

I think that maybe you don't all the time really understand children and they don't understand you. But you should try to understand them.

If they have problems, you should try to get to the bottom of them. If you see something that's wrong with them, you should inquire about it and ask what's going on in their minds. When I was coming up, no one ever bothered about asking me anything. It was just—if you spoke, you spoke, and if you didn't, you didn't. And that would be one way in which I wouldn't bring children up because that annoys me.

There's nothing I would keep because of the fact that I disapprove of my child life, of my whole upbringing. I wouldn't keep anything as of right now. There is nothing, right now. If I were telling somebody about raising children and I didn't have any of my own and the only experience I would have had was living with my mother and father—well, I wouldn't advise them because, actually, I wouldn't know. And I'd know that whatever I do wouldn't be right, so I wouldn't say anything.

Mrs. Todd's facility in expressing her thoughts about child rearing was tied in with her own sense of past and present deprivations. She wanted "something different" for her children, yet her background experiences and present resources did not prepare her to offer them that something different. She knew how she thought family life and child rearing should be, but she did not think she could bring it about.

It was probably this awareness of the gap between what

she said and what she did that made her say she did not consider herself such a good mother.

Emotional care: "not to cuddlesome." Mrs. Todd's relationship with her children was marked by a seeming diffidence and reluctance to respond to them emotionally. She was undemonstrative most of the time. When nine-month-old Shirley would tug at her skirt to be picked up or would try to sit on her lap, Mrs. Todd would usually push her away roughly, saying, "Get away from me, I'm not your mother," or, "Don't always be calling me Mama."

On one occasion Mrs. Todd told about one of her visits to an acquaintance in the building. As she entered the apartment, she overheard the mother criticizing her to a neighbor for not being affectionate to children.

"I didn't get angry," said Mrs. Todd. "I just said, 'You're right!'"

Mrs. Todd explained that her friend talked about her because she never picked children up; another acquaintance claimed that Mrs. Todd was the only one who came into her home who did not pick up the baby. Mrs. Todd asked:

Why should I pick up her child when I don't even pick up my own? But when I do go there, I always give some attention to the one she leaves in bed all day, as I don't think it's right to give all the attention to one child.

On another occasion when Mrs. Todd was asked to pick up her neighbor's crying baby, she refused and explained to me: "Maybe I'm funny, but I just don't believe in it."

Among the mothers, Mrs. Todd was not alone in her negative attitude about picking up children. I observed a similar reaction in my neighbor, Mrs. Norris, whose two-year-old son I sometimes picked up. One consequence was that, whenever he saw me, he came toward me expectantly and held out his arms to be picked up. If I did pick him up, he would sit contentedly clutching me around the neck. Often, in order to put him down, I had to pry his hands apart, so tight was his hold. When I told Mrs. Norris that her son seemed to like me, she said, "That's because you pick him up. You're spoiling him, and I'm not going to pick him up." Some mothers seemed to equate overt demonstrations of warmth and affection with spoiling.

A suggestion that this parental attitude got transferred to children came from Mrs. Todd's five-year-old daughter, Elsie. She had been playing with my son two days in succession. The second day, she asked me if my son was sick. Since my son was actively playing with her, I was puzzled and asked why she wanted to know this. "Well," she replied, "you were carrying him last night!" I then recalled that I had automatically picked my son up when he had fallen, hit his head and begun to cry. Elsie made no association between his fall and my picking him up. Apparently, in her experience, only a child's illness called for this behavior.

During my early association with Mrs. Todd, I was strongly tempted to apply the familiar psychological label of rejection to her refusal to pick up her children unless they were ill or incapacitated beyond any doubt. As time went on, this early temptation to apply a hackneyed label was weakened and eventually eliminated. I became much more uncertain about my diagnostic abilities in this and other matters.

I frequently found myself wondering why I could be so fond of a person who treated her children the way Mrs. Todd did. By the time I left the project, I wondered how she did so well. This change in my thinking about her child-rearing behavior was not due merely to the understanding that is likely to come with friendship.

My speculations about Mrs. Todd's behavior continued after I left the housing project. When I viewed her in the context of all the other mothers that we had observed and interviewed in the Child Rearing Study, a possible explanation of a real puzzle began to emerge. I think that there may be a basic difference between the mother who defines a good mother as loving and the mother who defines a good mother as "not too cuddlesome".

I think that the failure of the first type of mother to be loving is due to reasons that are different from those usually given for the failure of the second type of mother to be loving. The behavior of the first type of mother suggests the classical picture of rejection. But, if we attempt to describe the behavior of the second type of mother in the same way, we might be somewhat wide of the mark because we are judging her in the light of child-rearing values to which she gives different priority and weight. Other family values might take precedence.

In Mrs. Todd's case, I think the child-rearing values which take precedence are those related to independence training. Some mothers seem to withhold affection not because they reject their children, but because they want to train their children away from depending on them. They are under pressure to get each child "out of the way" as soon as possible in order to go on to the next child. But, in these terms, as well as in the mothers' views, the response to these pressures is not rejection. This is, perhaps, why Mrs. Todd could point to the paradox of her friend criticizing her for not picking up her children but complimenting her on how nice a child Mrs. Todd's nine-month-old daughter was.

Independence training: being on your own early. One evening, Mrs. Todd was seated at our kitchen table with Helen, drinking hot tea. When her youngest daughter, Shirley, tugged at her skirts for a drink of the tea, Mrs. Todd held the cup to her daughter's lips, but the heat of the cup made the child flinch. The following interchange occurred:

Helen: Don't give her that hot tea! She'll burn herself.
Mrs. T: That's the only way for her to learn what it means. When she sees it's hot, she'll leave it alone.

Annoyed by what she had seen and by the exchange with Mrs. Todd, Helen got up and drew a glass of water from the kitchen faucet for Shirley. She held the glass as the child drank thirstily.

Mrs. T: (*pretending to address her daughter*) I'm going to leave you with Helen, because she's making it hard for me.

Helen: What do you mean? She's thirsty! I only gave her some water.

Mrs. T: But you didn't have to hold the glass! She knows how to hold a cup.

Mrs. Todd believed in early training in everything. Her last child, Shirley, was toilet trained in less time than any of the others. She stressed having her children learn to feed and dress themselves early. At less than a year, Shirley was seated at the table with her brothers and sister, perched on a pile of books, with a plate of food before her just like the rest. It was also true that at the ages of two and three, Mrs. Todd's children had made considerable progress in dressing themselves. Her three-year-old son, Nicholas, could tie his shoe laces, and my four-year-old son could not. It did not matter to Mrs. Todd that a child's shirt was on backwards; the point was that the child had put it on.

Mrs. Todd thought it scandalous that the parent who criticized her for not picking up her children did not permit her own children to dress themselves, especially since the oldest child would soon be going to kindergarten. Once when Mrs. Todd was in this parent's home and was asked to help dress the children, Mrs. Todd tested them out by handing them each an article of clothing to put on. She found out, to her satisfaction, that the children could dress themselves, if need be, and this made her friend's behavior inexcusable.

On more than one occasion, I saw Mrs. Todd demonstrate skill and patience in teaching a child how to do something. One of her demonstrations, which I shall not soon forget, involved me.

My son and Phillip, her four-year-old, had been wrestling on the floor on a blanket. When they finished wrestling and started on some other activity, I arose to pick the blanket up.

"Sit down!" Mrs. Todd said firmly, and I obeyed instantly. "Let me show you how to do it," she said, as she called the boys and had them spread the blanket out smoothly on the floor. Without moving from her chair and never changing her tone of voice, she gave clear, concise, step-by-step instructions to each of the children. This one was to take this corner and bring it to that corner, and that one was to take the other corner and bring it to this corner. The children followed her instructions with ease, and my son's pride in his accomplishment made me chagrined at my hastiness in assuming the responsibility.

Baby sitting was another child-rearing role which Mrs. Todd began teaching her children early. She taught her three-, four-, and five-year-olds how to dress and feed the baby.

In spite of the fact that Mrs. Todd complained of the child-rearing responsibility for her own brothers and sisters that she had had as a child, she appeared to be giving her children the same kind of responsibility. Her five-year-old daughter, Elsie, was given a major baby-sitting responsibility. Mrs. Todd would sometimes leave all the children in Elsie's charge for two and three hours at a time. She gave Elsie authority to hit the other children with a ruler if they misbehaved; the other children seemed to recognize that to go against their sister was tantamount to going against their mother. Elsie, sometimes tyrannical in her rule, handled easily the discipline of her younger brothers and sisters; yet, she was just a year or two older than the others.

Possibly as a result of Elsie's "Little Mother" role, a very close relationship developed between her and three-year-old brother Nicholas. He went to her with his injuries and problems, often even if his mother was at home. The ties between the two became so strong that they caused Mrs. Todd to refer to the trouble she was having trying to "get Nicholas away from [five-year-old] Elsie" because the latter "had him so tight".

Control: making them mind. According to Mrs. Todd, her husband had been the disciplinarian in the family. She could mimic the way he would bark "Attention!" to call the children to order as though he were giving a military command. But she was aware that there were other aspects of her husband's relationships with the children:

I don't say anything; they are his children, but his mother and father say that he is mean. That's all right, they love him. In fact, they like him better than they like me.

Mrs. Todd saw that the absence of her husband imposed added responsibilities for discipline upon her. The following excerpts are from a taped interview:

I don't think you should keep them under lock and key, and I don't think you should let them run free. I think you should punish them when they are wrong. I don't think you should have to beat them or say that you are going to kill them. Taking away a privilege sometimes seems to me better than beating them. I don't think that a whipping really works on children no more than I think taking their privileges do because they are human beings just like anybody else. I feel that if it were someone over me that said, 'If you don't do this, I'm not going to give you a doll,' or, 'I'm not going to give you your allowance,' I would say, 'Well, it doesn't matter to me whether you give it to me or not, I'll get it some other way.' Or, if they would beat me, I would probably be so used to beatings, I'd say, 'Well, you get a beating and it's over with and then you go ahead do whatever you want to do anyway.'

I think maybe understanding from the beginning would be better than beatings or taking away privileges. You could understand them, and they could understand you. And they would know right from wrong just bringing them up like that. But some are born to be good, and others are born to be bad.

I don't always think that it's in the upbringing because, if you just have something on your mind and you want to be bad, well, you just strive to be bad. If you want to be good and make something of yourself, well, you strive for that. It just seems that some children from the beginning, they just be bad and are just like that all the rest of their life no matter what kind of guidance they have had through their life. Other people are good all through their life, well, they seem to be good.

Some people say, 'That little boy, he so bad he'll prob-

ably grow up and be some hoodlum or something.'
I don't know whether I am contradicting myself in
saying it, but all the time it just doesn't work out that
way. He might grow up to be a preacher and the one
that was good might grow up to be a hoodlum.

But just like I said, it might not be in the upbringing of
the child. It might just be in the child's mind and something happened along the way that made him want
to change.

The above represents one of the many instances in which
Mrs. Todd tried to sort out her experiences and thoughts
about child rearing. Not only were uncertainties apparent
in what she said, but it was also clear that she had not been
able to put into consistent practice some of the child-rearing methods she thought constructive. She controlled not
through understanding but through fear. She demanded
almost instant obedience and exacted it through whipping
the children and frequently by screeching at the top of her
voice. Her screeches were piercing and spine-tingling; their
penetrating suddenness never failed to galvanize me.

There were occasions when I saw her children stopped
dead in their tracks just at the shrill sound of their names;
they would drop whatever they were doing and hasten to
see what was wanted. Mrs. Todd's characteristic demand
was for instant compliance, and she generally got it. Some
times she would line the children up on the sofa and dare
them to move. There they sat like frozen little statues; fear,
anxiety and consternation were written all over their faces.

Mrs. Todd showed some awareness of the questionable
nature of her behavior in controlling the children. One day
she knew that I was aware of her beating one of the children since he had screamed so loud. Later in the day, she
said that she guessed I thought she was beating him half
to death. When I told her that was the way it sounded, she
mentioned that four-year-old Phillip had poured a cupful
of dirt in the baby's crib. She said reflectively that she just
did not know what to make of him; she was looking forward to her husband's return at which time she would turn
Phillip over to him.

From time to time, Mrs. Todd made remarks which indicated her opinion that Phillip was a child "born to be bad." The "born to be bad" theme was not unique to Mrs. Todd. Certainly the black sheep is not a new idea.* As noted earlier, Mrs. Martin had voiced a similar opinion, and I encountered variations on the concept in field interviews. According to Mrs. Todd, Phillip was more aggressive than her other children and could not be trusted. He was constantly getting into difficulty because of his bizarre (disturbed?) behavior. On one occasion he set fire to a bedspread. Another time, when I was baby sitting with him in the court, he picked up an empty Clorox bottle and suddenly smashed it on the sidewalk.

Sometimes Mrs. Todd referred to him as being "not all there". She cited the following incident: one day Phillip had come to her complaining that he had nothing to do. Exasperated that he would say this when she had just gotten him toys for Christmas, she told him to go bump his head against the wall in his room. He not only did this but returned to her saying he was tired of doing it and asking for something else to do. Still annoyed, Mrs. Todd told him to go and bump his head against the other wall.

Mrs. Todd ended her story with an amazed, "And do you know that he did it!"

Providing the basic necessities: priorities and problems. My experience at the housing project taught me that it is no small accomplishment for low-income families to provide "decent food, clothing and shelter". I came to realize why so many mothers in and outside the project considered the provision of adequate physical care a major, if not the major, aspect of good motherhood. Adequate physical care could not be taken for granted, and seeing that the children got food, clothing and shelter was sometimes quite a feat. Different mothers had different physical-care prob-

* The black-sheep idea is a part of our American heritage. I think that we may not realize the extent to which this idea is still held. There are still those who believe that there is such a thing as an intrinsically bad child and that his badness was not of the parents' making. It may well be that some of the children who get written off early in life, as Mrs, Todd appears to have written off this son, are the ones thought "born to be bad."

lems, and these differences usually affected priorities.

With Mrs. Todd, rent had first priority among physical-care categories. She was determined to keep the roof over their heads until her husband got back. The rent bill was the first thing she paid when she got her allotment, even though she did not always have enough money left to meet other needs.

Clothing was one of these needs. Trying to keep her four children clothed was a critical problem. One way of easing it was to develop different styles of dress to fit varied situations. For example, Mrs. Todd had four clothing levels for her children, ranging from complete undress to Sunday best.

One day I knocked on Mrs. Todd's door and found her five-year-old daughter in charge of what looked like a small nudist colony. Since it was somewhat chilly, I asked Elsie if she didn't think it was too cold for the baby and, without hesitation, she replied, "That's the way my mother wants her."

Mrs. Todd, like other mothers, frequently let her children run naked around the house. Sometimes the reason they were stripped was that it was wash day and there was nothing extra to put on while their clothes were being washed. At other times, the nakedness of a small child could be due to the heat or to efforts to save clean clothes for more public occasions.

Now and then I found the children, particularly baby Shirley, in semi-dress, wearing an undershirt but no panties. This was a pervasive pattern of dress for small children. At first I did not know how to interpret this semi-dress; I found mothers, who exhibited high standards for their children's welfare, dressing (or not dressing) their children in the same way. The more I saw of Mrs. Todd and other families, the more a relatively simple explanation for the practice began to take shape in my mind. Families just did not have the quantity of diapers and training pants needed for children who were not yet completely toilet trained. When funds were limited, priority had to be given to the purchase of outer clothing rather than underwear.

One result of this semi-dress was frequent urine puddles on the floor and I heard one exasperated mother cry, "I'm sick of wiping up this pissy floor." One mother had an alternative to floor wiping; she passed this job on to her children. Once when this mother's four-year-old son reported in an alarming voice that the baby had "made doo-doo" on the floor, the mother said, "Well, you know what to do; get a rag and clean it up."

Sometimes Mrs. Todd's children were dirty and disheveled. I never knew whether their appearance on these occasions was due to a lack of money to buy soap powder or to Mrs. Todd's low spirits. Either explanation could have been right. I observed, however, that when the children were dirty, Mrs. Todd was careful to see that they stayed in the building and played only in the house or in the hall. Going outside was a different matter; she always made them more presentable then. As she put it, she wanted them to look decent enough so people wouldn't talk about the way she kept her children.

This concern about what other people had to say about their children was pervasive among the mothers. In general, children who came into the court to play looked presentable. I noticed, for example, that raggedy and unkempt children were much more in evidence within a block or two of the project, in areas that were still physically deteriorated.

Proximate living in the project appeared to have been a factor in many efforts to conform to better standards of public dress for their children and, to a lesser degree, for themselves.

When Mrs. Todd's children left the grounds of the housing project, she made a special effort to dress them as well as she could. Once Mrs. Todd refused an invitation to take Phillip on an automobile trip to the airport because he had "nothing to wear". When she was pressed for an explanation, she said that the clothing he had was not suitable enough for him to go. It was only after a neighbor lent him some pants and socks that she let him go. When she took her children to visit relatives, they would be clean and neat. She took special pains to see that they looked their best whenever they went to her mother's house in a middle class residential neighborhood. For their out-of-town vacation trip to visit relatives in a nearby state, she bought each child a completely new outfit.

Mrs. Todd managed the problem of clothing the children as well as she did only because of help from family and friends. She received hand-me-downs for her daughters from a sister who had several girls. When Phillip, her older son, outgrew the few clothes he had, they were passed down to Nicholas. Keeping Phillip adequately clothed was Mrs. Todd's biggest clothing problem; she had no ready-made or easy source of hand-me-downs for him. Occasionally her mother-in-law furnished items of clothing for the various children, particularly for Elsie, who seemed to be her favorite. From time to time, Mrs. Todd's mother gave her dresses for the girls. Friends in the project would also give her clothing that their children had outgrown. Despite her children's clothing needs, Mrs. Todd thought about helping others. She asked if I might know some family among those in CRS's study group that could use her youngest daughter's hand-me-downs.

Ranking second among the basic things Mrs. Todd wanted for her children was "decent food". This was a chronic need and made for continuing frustration. She tried to stay abreast of things by juggling the regular expected income and the hoped-for extra money from her husband. One month she would pay all the bills with her allotment and buy food with any extra money that her husband sent. The next month she would use her allotment to store up on food and rely on the extra money expected from her husband to pay bills. However, this juggling act failed when no extra money came from Mr. Todd.

Mrs. Todd's food standards and tastes were relatively high as measured by the cheaper and inferior fare offered in some neighborhood stores. She scorned the neighborhood stores that regularly slipped handbills under the apartment doors advertising their weekly specials. The prices sounded more like Depression prices than 1960 prices—for example, four pounds of fish for $1, five pounds of chicken backs for 59 cents, three pounds of chicken wings for 98 cents, pork chops at 39 cents a pound, liver at three pounds for 49 cents. For 89 cents, you could get a breakfast special consisting of one pound of sausage meat, one dozen eggs, one stick of margarine and one can of biscuits.

Mrs. Todd said that she would not buy any old thing to feed her children as neither they nor she were used to cheap foods. Describing a breakfast that the Todds had one day when a visiting friend purchased the food, she said, "We had bacon, eggs, grits and biscuits," and added, "One day my children eat like kings, and the next day they have nothing."

Her children liked to have two eggs apiece, and, with her income and its ups and downs, it took too many eggs for one such breakfast. She said that, occasionally, she gave them each one egg, but it took her a day or two to make up the expense for this kind of breakfast. The children were much more apt to get a dish of cereal or grits.

Mrs. Todd preferred to do her shopping at a commissary for service men and their families where food was cheaper. Unless she had someone to drive her there she could not save enough to make a trip to the commissary worthwhile because the round trip taxi fare wiped out any savings. Several times when she was offered a ride, she refused, saying that she had so little money to spend that it was not worth going so far.

Their diet was generally starchy, with emphasis on beans, spaghetti, noodles and potatoes. The children were particularly fond of canned meat balls and spaghetti; she gave this to them quite frequently. Another frequent meal was frozen fish sticks and frozen French fries. It was not that Mrs. Todd did not know how to prepare a balanced meal; it rather was that she chronically lacked the money and, frequently, the incentive to do it.

Often, Mrs. Todd went without meals herself because she did not like the food that she gave the children. Now and then, long after the children had gone to sleep, she would treat herself to a small, treasured piece of steak.

Numerous, undramatic little events taught me the meaning of hunger. Some lessons in hunger were provided unwittingly by the Todd children. For example, a bowl of fruit usually stood on my dinette table. When Mrs. Todd's children came over to play, they would eye it longingly and sometimes ask for an apple or a banana. As we became more friendly, their requests increased with the frequency of their visits. First, I tried to regulate demand and supply by keeping the fruit elsewhere. I began to notice that when the children came over, they would eventually make their way to the kitchen; and there, their eyes would roam around the room as though looking for something. It began to dawn on me that the fruit was less a snack or treat than a supplement to, or even a substitute for, a meal. It was an important means of appeasing the hunger that was such a constant part of the lives of many children in the project.

One day I found Mrs. Todd's nine-month-old Shirley picking dirt off the wheels of a child's tricycle and eating it. I was so startled that I shouted at her to stop. Mrs. Todd came to see what the trouble was. Her daughter did not stop for me nor did she stop the first time her mother spoke to her. Finally, Mrs. Todd had to pick the dirt out of the girl's mouth. When I asked if Mrs. Todd had ever seen her daughter eat dirt before, she said that she had seen her pick the dirt off her brother Phillip's tricycle and eat it. She was at a loss to explain Shirley's behavior.*

On one occasion Mrs. Todd described a food fantasy she often had, one involving her teen-age brothers and sisters: she imagined she had taken them on a beach picnic and had so much hot food cooked up that they were able to eat all they wanted.

She followed this image with: "Can you imagine a loaf of bread lasting two days with six children?" When I showed some doubt, she said, "Well it did in my house because my mother wouldn't permit us to touch it unless she gave it to us. We would get a beating if we did."

Such expressions of Mrs. Todd's feelings, thoughts, and memories involving food helped me understand better what seemed to be a contradiction in her behavior toward her

---

* This particular instance of "hunger" is probably best classified as an example of what is medically called *pica*.

children. Relying on what I thought I knew about Mrs. Todd, I had fully expected her to get angry when I saw her children go into the groceries she had brought home one day and eat a loaf of bread before she got a chance to put the rest of the purchases away. Instead of anger or annoyance, she showed the opposite, pleasure and permissiveness. It appeared that hunger was one of her children's experiences with which she readily identified. This same permissiveness and lack of anger, in matters where food for her children was involved, showed in her amusement when a three-layer cake she had baked disappeared in two hours.

One of her often repeated wishes was to be able to set one loaf in front of each of her children and let them eat until they had had their fill of bread—at least once.

Despite the trouble she had providing adequate food, Mrs. Todd was reluctant to acknowledge how bad at times the situation was for her. Some of the facts and many of the dimensions of her family's food story came out only gradually. Some were revealed in situations like the following:

One day she interrupted a conversation to ask if I had ever heard of anybody filling up on ice cream when hungry. When I asked why anybody would make such an odd choice, she replied, "Well, when that's all you can get on your Central Charge Account, ice cream is better than nothing, and with a few cup cakes you can make a meal."

When I pressed to find out whether she was saying obliquely that she had no food, she insisted that she had food. The next day she mentioned that she was thinking about asking to be referred to Surplus Foods by the agency from which she was asking help with the beds. I told her that she could make an application to Surplus Foods without an agency referral and offered to take her there. She said she could do this the following week since she had to remain at home for a few days, waiting for a visit from a social worker with information about the beds.

The following day when I came home from work, Mrs. Todd was waiting for me. Hearing my key in the latch, she poked her head out of her door and asked if I was too tired to do her a favor: she wanted to go to a Peoples Drug

Store. Recalling her comment about filling up on ice cream, I immediately offered my services and took her to the drug store. The bulky bag she came out with looked like it might contain ice cream, and I also caught a whiff of tomato soup. Mrs. Todd offered no explanations.

On our return home, I mentioned that I was going to the A&P grocery and asked if she wanted anything. "I don't have any money," she said. "I'm expecting some tomorrow. If I don't get it, I will probably have to go over to my mother's." I asked what she needed but she replied, "Nothing. I have things at home. It's just that I never have everything at one time to make something."

I asked her what she needed in order to make something. She again refused to acknowledge any need at first, but after a pause she blurted, "You can bring me a loaf of day-old bread." I said that I didn't know what she planned to make out of the bread but there must be something else she needed. She delayed answering and then said, "Well if you just want to be real nice, bring me anything!"

As we separated, she asked if my son could come over and have some ice cream.

Mrs. Todd did receive some money from her husband the next day. The following week she asked me to take her to apply for surplus food. Perhaps some of the significance this trip had for her—and for me—came through in her wry but warm remark when we returned home: "Thank you, Mother, for taking me there."

When she eventually got her first supplies from Surplus Foods, she immediately offered some to me. The following week, however, she was in the doldrums again. I did not see her or the children for two successive days. The second evening of her two days of being incommunicado, she telephoned to say that she had decided that she had better call her mother (meaning me) and tell me where she was as she knew that I would be worried. She had no food in the house so she had taken all the children and gone to her mother-in-law's home.

These incidents and exchanges give some idea of the inconsistent way things went for Mrs. Todd—a good meal, a slim meal, no meals. But, somehow, she made it; and, despite circumstances, bursts of enthusiastic creativity would occasionally flare up.

One Easter, I shared some Easter egg dye with her. She later came over to borrow "any kind of flavoring" I had and invited me to see the cake she was making. When I went to Mrs. Todd's apartment, the children were gathered around the table, intently watching as she put finishing touches on the cake. She had tinted some coconut brown and formed it into a basket which nested in grass of green-tinted coconut on white icing. In the basket were several jelly beans representing Easter eggs. In addition to the cake, there was an impressive roasted turkey. The children were looking on excitedly and anticipating their out-of-the-ordinary meal. Everything was pleasant and harmonious. *

In general, Mrs. Todd was very interested in food and its preparation. She could watch someone prepare a dish she had never cooked before and then duplicate it with no difficulty. She used to joke that her husband would not know what had happened when he returned home, and she would prepare new dishes like chili and chop suey she had learned to prepare as a result of watching and listening to me.

Mrs. Todd was also interested in the proper service of food. One day she was present when I was setting the table for guests and began helping me. When she asked me where the salad plates were, I told her that I did not feel like dirtying so many dishes and was not going to use them. With a disdainful grunt, she overruled me, got out the salad plates and, as if to silence any protest I might have had, told me that she would come back and do the dishes. *

Getting an education: to benefit the world. Mrs. Todd left school when she was in the twelfth grade to get married. She said that going to school had not been a particu-

* It was this kind of experience that led me to be leery of the easy and sometimes automatic label, "maternal rejection," for a mother like Mrs. Todd.
* I have often wondered whether Mrs. Todd was really saying to me, "I might have to use jelly glasses to drink out of in my house, but if you have salad plates in your house, then there is no reason to act as if you do not have any. I use what I've got, why don't you do the same thing?"

larly pleasant experience; frequently, she had to go without food and adequate clothing. She received fifty cents a week for lunch money. When her clothes were burned in a fire in her home and not replaced; she had to wear what she could of her sisters' clothing. When she took courses like interpretive dancing and drama, she never had money to buy costumes and other necessary equipment. She finally became disgusted because such lacks prevented her from taking part in many activities.

Mrs. Todd had liked school and wished she had been able to finish high school. The fact that her brother was now in college and doing well gave her some vicarious pleasure.

History had been her favorite subject; she had taken it every semester. She had had three years of typing and some courses in operating office machines. Frequently she would assist a neighbor in her lessons by dictating to her for speed-writing practice. Occasionally, Mrs. Todd would borrow my typewriter; she would always show me what she had typed when she returned it.

In speaking about the education of her own children, Mrs. Todd gave the same kind of cautiously hopeful answer that many of the mothers in the Child Rearing Study gave:

As long as they are interested in it, they should go on and do whatever they want to. College, if you have the money, or a part-time job to help work their way through college. I don't think I would force my children to go to college, or anywhere else, because it would be useless spending your money to force them to go. I just wouldn't force them to do anything that they wouldn't want to do after they finish high school. If they wanted to go to college I would try to help them if I could. If they didn't, I would guide them into what they wanted to do, but they should finish high school.

Mrs. Todd showed active interest in providing support and some enrichment for her children's present education:

I've joined the book club, those read-by-myself books,

so that I can read them to Elsie and she'll know more about them. I guess that if I read them to her and she knew about them, it would make her more alert when she got in school and the teacher was reading them to the kids. The only other thing is that we bought her a set of encyclopedias, but that isn't too beneficial to her now. By the time she gets ready to use them she will probably have a need for more because I guess they would be too old.

In terms of careers, she repeated the high aspirations for at least one of her children that are recurrent among the parents CRS came to know:

I think they should become what they want to become. But I would like to see one become a biochemist, because that's what I had on my mind at one time—or something that would be beneficial to the world today —some sort of field where there aren't many people working but they need more in that field.

In encouraging her children's development (and independence) Mrs. Todd seemed to be at her best and most consistent.

She acted upon her belief that every child should have some preschool training by putting her children in the half-day nursery school that was operated by the Recreation Department. She said she wanted much more than the school could give. She expressed her disappointment in the Mothers' Club, composed of mothers of children in the nursery school. As she saw it, instead of talking about what to do about the children, the mothers who attended the meetings of the Mothers' Club spent their time gossiping. She said they were interested in only two things, "trying to outdo the others and trying to keep the women away from their husbands".

She said that she used to play with her children a lot, teaching them various things, and she would always read to them at night before they went to bed. The result of her instruction showed. Her oldest daughter, Elsie, could read at a third-grade level when she completed first grade. Elsie was interested in books; whenever she visited, the first thing she did was to go to the bookshelf and then sit and read one book after another. She was very alert. So was her younger brother, Nicholas, who was so closely attached to her. He showed that he had picked up quite a bit from her. At the age of three, he knew the alphabet and could count; and he was better than his four-year-old brother at recognizing colors.

A part of the problem Mrs. Todd had in preparing her children for starting school was getting enough clothing for them. She sent her children to relatives in the South for the summer as part of her plan to free herself for summer work in order to earn money to buy their clothes.

Mr. Todd was also aware of the continuing pressure and threat exerted by the need to get clothing for children. In a letter to his wife, he expressed understanding that she might not be able to feed them properly, but that she should concentrate on getting them clothing for school even if they had to eat beans every day.*

On an occasion when we were making a tape recording of the children to send to her husband, Mrs. Todd skillfully guided and encouraged responses from the small children. She worked patiently with them to overcome their fear of the machine. She was very proud when they finally came through with their recitations: nursery rhymes, The Lord's Prayer, and the Pledge of Allegiance to the flag.

Mrs. Todd's displays of marked potential for being a better than ordinary mother, wife and human being sparked occasionally but, seemingly, never had the opportunity to develop fully and to be sustained. That they did not develop fully and were not sustained in Mrs. Todd's case—

* My observation of this struggle to get adequate clothing for school made me wonder whether, in much of the speculation and theory about the failure of low-income parents to motivate their children, we may be overlooking an important factor. Many of these parents remember from their own experience that their motivation was dulled by the lack of adequate clothing and sufficient food. Therefore, they see these needs as essential and much of their energy is absorbed in trying to meet these elementary needs. Perhaps they remember, too, that without some minimum sense of physical well-being, it is useless to worry about academic motivation.

as in that of many of the mothers—was clearly one of the consequences of not enough money and of the uneven flow of available money.

Added Specifics of Child Rearing: Mrs. Queene

Mrs. Queene, the mother who felt her chances for development when an adolescent had been sacrificed by her parents for a car, had two children, five-year-old Elaine, and four-year-old Tony. She wanted another child and had been trying to get pregnant for over a year. She had even been to a fertility clinic. Before I left the project, her third child was on the way.

Mrs. Queene presented a somewhat different picture from that of Mrs. Todd in her child-rearing behavior. One source of that difference was the involvement of Mrs. Queene's children in her marital problems. Still, Mr. and Mrs. Queene shared a basic wish and general desire to do more for their children than their parents had done for them.

When asked if she was raising her children the same way she had been raised, Mrs. Queene replied:

No-o-o. But maybe so, in one instance. I find myself sometimes arguing like my mother did, and this is wrong; it's the only fault I find with myself. When I was coming up, I was often hungry, never had lunch money, and never had enough clothes. . . .

Emotional care: love and trust. Mrs. Queene was quite demonstrative toward her children, although there was considerable unevenness in her behavior. Her child-rearing emphasis was on love, while Mrs. Todd's was on independence training. (I would often wonder how much this difference in child-rearing emphases or priorities was related to the fact that Mrs. Queene had only two children and Mrs. Todd had four.)

When I asked Mrs. Queene what she thought was the most important thing about raising children nowadays, she repeated the love theme. Whipping played a counterpoint to the love theme in her reply:

A child should know that you do love him. Now take Elaine, for instance. She lies a little and I tries to get her to talk. I tell her that she should not be afraid to tell me anything as I am her mother. No matter what she does she should tell me, and I will not whip her. Sometimes she will start to deny something and catch herself and go ahead and tell me the truth. Now that she knows the what and whys, she is doing better. I guess I would say love and trust.

When I asked Mrs. Queene what she thought were the most important things a child should have, she immediately asked if I was talking about material things. When given the option of replying in terms of either material things or nonmaterial things, she chose nonmaterial things—affection and praise:

Well, take Elaine. She likes a lot of affection. She is always sitting around right under me. I guess this is because she got a lot of affection when she was a baby. She likes praise when she does things. I always try to praise her and kiss her when she does something good.

After several months of intermittent conversations, we got around to discussing her interest in having another child. By then I knew her well enough to ask her why she would want another child when she was constantly talking of separating from her husband. Her reply gave another intimation of the emotional involvement of her children in her marital problems:

I don't rightfully know. I guess it's because I like doing things for it, nursing it and washing for it. Then it keeps me busy; it keeps my mind off things. I used to just sit down and think a lot, but if I'm busy I don't have time to think. Maybe it's because of the affection I don't get from [my husband] and I will get from the baby.

80

Scapegoating her husband seemed a daily occurrence with Mrs. Queene. She showed no hesitation in discussing her marital problems in the presence of her children, whether she was talking with someone on the phone or face-to-face. Arguments with her husband occurred in the children's presence. In some of these, she would let loose a stream of verbal abuse, calling him "dumb and stupid", and punctuating the abuse with profanity. She badgered him constantly about the fact that he would never take the children with him when he went out.

The children had a tendency to take sides. Elaine acted as if she identified with her mother, and Tony seemed to identify with his father. Elaine would parrot her mother's chronic complaints on occasions when she chastised her father: "God will punish you for hurting us like this." Once she told me, as if she were confiding something: "Maybe God will help Daddy to think about how he is hurting us."

Tony, when he saw his father leaving the house on one occasion, said to him: "We won't have a daddy if you go."

Mrs. Queene readily acknowledged that her husband was "crazy about" the children, yet she did not believe that this was enough. He should show them how much he liked them by doing more things for and with them.

She appeared threatened by her son's attachment to his father and seemed to resent Tony's immediate rush to see his father when he awakened in the mornings. Apparently more disturbing to her was Tony's reaction when she confronted him with the need to choose between her and her husband in the event they separated. To her dismay, Tony's preference was to go with his father. Mrs. Queene's retort was that this would happen only over her dead body.

Control: whipping on the spot. While Mrs. Queene may not have whipped Elaine for telling lies, she showed no reluctance to whip her children for other behavior when she disapproved of it. Her threats to "whip your butt" or "whip your behind" were frequent, and she prided herself on carrying out her threats. For example, once she meted out instant punishment when Elaine stamped her foot at her in the street, stopping then and there to spank the child.

On one occasion when I was visiting Mrs. Queene, she became quite annoyed with Tony who was running playfully and noisily from room to room and under tables and chairs. When she sent him to his room for not obeying her order to stop, it bothered her that he showed no contrition. "I don't know what's getting into them," she said in a puzzled manner, and then added, "They are getting harder to control." She cited a recent instance in which Elaine had left for school without her permission. Mrs. Queene warned Elaine that a repetition of such behavior would result in her coming to school and whipping Elaine in front of her class.

Actually, Mrs. Queene's children did not give the impression of being difficult to control. My personal speculation was that her almost chronic complaining about minor infractions of her rules and expectations was related primarily to her increasing insecurity in handling different stages in the children's development. She preferred taking care of babies. In this respect she reminded me of other mothers who expressed similar concern and uncertainty when a child began to have "a mind of his own".*

Providing the basics: regular income makes a difference. Mrs. Queene's emphasis on physical care showed itself early in her children's upbringing. One of her reasons for wanting another child was the satisfaction she got in caring for babies: she loved to "keep their clothes clean and see nice white diapers hanging on the line". Because of the regularity of her husband's weekly earnings, she did not have to worry about food, and meeting the rent bill was no problem so long as her husband did not "mess up" on the money. Her husband's steady income may help to explain why and how she was able to put a good bit of interest and energy into clothing her children and caring for their clothes.

Mrs. Queene's children were among the best-dressed children in the court. Pert Elaine was a familiar sight in

---

* There may be certain critical points in the child-rearing process in which either the parent or the child sets in motion a kind of social weaning. In Mrs. Queene's case, it seemed to begin when her children showed signs of becoming independent personalities. With Mrs. Todd, it began when she put her children down to walk.

her dainty dresses and layers of starched petticoats; she acted as if she were quite conscious of how nice she looked. Nor was Tony outdone; in his matching shirts and shorts he seemed to glory in riding his two-wheeled bike, the largest in the court. All this "ostentation" was too much for Mrs. Harris, the court dowager, who criticized Mrs. Queene for overdressing her children for play.

Clothing her children in this fashion, I was certain, had a special meaning for Mrs. Queene; she was providing for her children what she herself had not had. And I am just as certain she was able to do it because the regularity of family income made a significant difference.

Getting an education: to do better than us. The oldest of six children, Mrs. Queene spoke about her childhood deprivations with evident feeling: often she had had to go to school hungry and had had no money to buy lunch at school. Sometimes classmates would bring lunch for her. She showed anger and resentment as she talked about the inadequacy of her school clothing. "Would you believe it?" she said, "I have never owned a pair of boots; I've never had an umbrella!"

Because she could no longer stand going to school under these circumstances, she dropped out of school in her junior year of high school.

There seemed to be a direct relationship between Mrs. Queene's emphasis on the physical care of her children and her active memories of going to school on an empty stomach and without proper clothing. There appeared to be a comparable relationship between her interest in her children's education and her memories of her school days. She was trying to plan ahead for her children's education and had taken out endowment policies on them two years before. It was touch-and-go keeping the policies up, but, thus far, she had not let them lapse.

Both she and her husband encouraged Elaine in her school work. Mrs. Queene reported with pride:

Elaine loves to write. I think she is going to be very smart. Some days she brings her *Weekly Reader* home and we do the work at home since they didn't get a chance to do it in school. I'm proud of her, and you should see how she can memorize things.

I think she is going to be very smart. I don't know where she gets it from as [my husband] doesn't have any education, and I was slow in school.

Parents inside and outside the housing project were usually positive in their educational hopes and plans for their children despite frequent negative feelings about their own circumstances. Mrs. Queene was no exception.

Her repeated indications that she was trying to provide something different in her children's school experience loom sharply as a counter theme to her frequent references to her own bitterness, despair and futility.

You know, I have begged God to take me away from here. . . .

I wonder how long do you have to suffer before something good happens. It just seems like I never have anything to look back to. . . .

My grandmother says that some good has to come. God is not going to put more on you than you can bear. . . . In a way, I believe what my grandmother says, but I know I don't have the faith I should have. I know it's a sin to pray like this, but sometimes I pray that my husband would get hurt like he has hurt me.

I know that this is praying for revenge and that I should not do it, but I don't want my children to come up like I did. I want them to go to school looking neat—well, I was always neat—I mean going to school with enough clothes to wear.

Added Specifics of Child Rearing: Mrs. Martin

Mrs. Martin, separated from her husband and the mother of four children (the last of whom was born out of wedlock),* struck me as a spirited, outgoing young woman. She and Mrs. Queene were quite friendly, but she quietly feuded with Mrs. Todd over the minor clashes that occurred among their children. Mrs. Martin was open in expressing her disapproval of both Mrs. Todd's child-rearing behavior and Mrs. Queene's attitude toward her husband. She was just as open in discussing her own behavior and attitudes, including the size of her family. In her characteristically dramatic way, one day she pointed an accusing finger at her two youngest children and said in pretended indignation:

> I tried to knock them out but I'm one of those people who just get pregnant quickly. I've tried to use a diaphragm but, the way I'm built, I can't use any of those and these [suppositories] don't do anything for you. . . . I got pregnant my first time, and I got Brenda my second time. That's the reason I'm scared of sex. I'm always afraid I'm going to get pregnant again.

Needs of children, as perceived. When I asked Mrs. Martin what she considered the most important thing or things about raising children nowadays, she shot back with lightening rapidity, "A mummy and both parents," thus defining her situation the way it was and the way she would have liked it to be. When asked what were the most important things a child should have, she answered:

> Food, clothes, medical care, a mama and a daddy. I guess a mother and a daddy come first—but if the children want food, they have to come to mother anyway, and if they need medical care they go to a doctor—so that's the way I see it, the way I gave it to you.

Like the other mothers, she said she wanted her child-rearing behavior to be an improvement over that of her parents. Asked whether she was bringing up her children the same way she was brought up, she said:

---

* Dorothy, age four; Brenda, age three; Tootsie, age two; Sharon, six months.

I'm trying to. No—that's not right. I'm not as strict. But when it comes to education, I'm hard on them; my father was hard on us about education.

So I'll be strict in education but not so strict in activities. I will also have more trust in my children. Daddy didn't have too much trust in us.

Emotional tones: "the bark is worse than the bite." Of these three mothers, Mrs. Martin impressed me as having the warmest personality. However, her attitude toward her children was a mixture of warmth and harshness; she was just as likely to be found screaming at them as cuddling and petting them. Sometimes the harshness was clearly only a pretense and, young as they were, the children seemed adept at figuring out when she was serious, and when she was not. Mrs. Martin and her children seemed to have a kind of communication that was not present in the relationships between the other two mothers and their children.

For example, we were seated outside the building and her five-year-old daughter, Dorothy, was leaning precariously over a railing above the basement stairway. Mrs. Martin screamed, "Dorothy, don't you know better than that? Come here!"

Dorothy stood speechless and wide-eyed in front of her mother and did not answer her.

"Don't you know better than that? Haven't I told you not to do anything like that? You'll fall and hurt yourself," complained Mrs. Martin. Dorothy maintained her silent stance.

Her temper rising, Mrs. Martin reached for one of the worn, felt bedroom slippers she was wearing and, in exasperation, jerked Dorothy across her lap. As she spanked her with the slipper, she said angrily, "Damn it, I ain't got no money to be taking you back and forth to the hospital!"

Dorothy responded with exaggerated howls until her mother released her, then stood whimpering in front of her mother.

"Go way!" commanded Mrs. Martin. "Get out of my sight with that crying!" Dorothy backed away a few begrudging steps and continued her subdued sobbing, her eyes fixed on her mother's face.

At Mrs. Martin's third repetition of her command, two-year-old Tootsie took matters into her hands and began pushing Dorothy away, whereupon Dorothy shoved Tootsie to the ground.

"Pick that child up!" cried Mrs. Martin, but Dorothy remained motionless. "Pick that child up off the ground!" demanded Mrs. Martin fiercely, as she patted her foot with deliberation.

Staunch in her opposition, Dorothy held her gaze and ignored her sister, who had by this time scrambled happily up.

A passing fire truck momentarily diverted our attention, and, when I turned, there was Dorothy huddled against her mother, still sobbing quietly. After ignoring her for a few minutes, Mrs. Martin then slowly slipped her arm around Dorothy and patted her gently.

Time and again, this mother's spontaneous warmth and affection followed and eased what I came to understand as pretended, superficial harshness and anger. Her children seemed to know that her bark was worse than her bite.

Independence training: teach them early. Mrs. Martin knew that her children displayed unusual independence— that "a whole lot of people" talked about the way she raised her children. She explained that, because of her lameness resulting from infantile paralysis, she had taught her children to do things early. When they were eight and nine months old she began teaching them how to pull up and down the stairs of the building, so that they could get to their third-floor apartment without her help.

At the age of two, Dorothy could go to the store by herself; Mrs. Martin would give her a note and watch her cross the street. She claimed that she could always count on Dorothy to perform errands properly. I have seen her send Dorothy, at the age of four, to the store with a note and a twenty-dollar bill. She showed not the slightest lack of confidence in Dorothy's ability to take care of the money.

For Mrs. Martin, Dorothy was the "outside type", the errand girl, but Brenda was different. She was the "house type". Mrs. Martin could rely on Brenda to help with the baby, change her diapers and fix her milk. Brenda was fond of the baby—a bubbling, outgoing infant, highly responsive to her sisters—and gladly took care of her. Dorothy was just the opposite.

All of the girls were taught to do housework. At times, when I stopped by their apartment, I would find Dorothy and Brenda busily cleaning, one with a broom and the other with a dust cloth. Two-year-old Tootsie was also pressed into service to pick up things off the floor. When I showed surprise that scrubbing the bathroom was included in the children's chores, Mrs. Martin said indignantly, "Who else is supposed to scrub it? They're the ones that dirties it up!"

One of the criticisms leveled by some neighbors against Mrs. Martin was that she left her children alone frequently. She scoffed at the implication that she was a neglecting mother, pointing out that she couldn't take four children with her every time she went to the store. She added quickly that she always notified neighbors when she left the house and asked them to look after the children. She acknowledged that, occasionally, the children did slip out of the house while she was gone. One day I found Brenda happily playing in the patio with not a stitch of clothing on. Mrs. Martin was shocked when I told her about this incident. She explained that she had gotten the children ready for a bath, and, finding she had no soap, had gone downstairs to borrow some from a friend. Brenda had slipped out of the apartment before her return.

Although Mrs. Martin related her emphasis on early independence training to her physical handicap, it is also probable that the close spacing of her four children had made such training almost necessary. She had to get one "out of the way" quickly in order to make way for the next one. Dorothy's responsiveness to independence training for outside activities as opposed to inside activities, which involved care of her younger sisters, may have been tied in with her reluctance to assume responsibilities for the younger sisters who had pushed her into the background.

Much of my observation leads me to speculate that in large low-income families, the older children occupy vulnerable positions; they have lessened opportunities for satisfactory relationships with their mothers. This is because of early independence training that is related to the rapid succession of siblings that makes demands not only upon their mothers but also upon them. The younger children in large low-income families can often find substitute relationships with older brothers and sisters that help compensate for the lacks in their parent-child relationship. This seemed to be true in the case of three-year-old Nicholas Todd who used his five-year-old sister as a mother substitute. His older brother was the isolate in the family.

A child's awareness of a mother's problem in handling several children was shown in Brenda's remark when Mrs. Martin, in doling out Kool-Aid to her children, overlooked her. Responding to the oversight, Brenda said, "Mother, have you forgotten you have another child?"

Control: theory and practice. When asked how tight she thought parents should be on children, Mrs. Martin replied:

That depends on their ages. A child five years old wouldn't do some of the things that an eleven-year-old child would do. But when mines gets to the first or second grade, I'm not gonna beat on them.

They do pretty good now. Take Dorothy. She marked on the wall with some crayon, but I didn't beat her. Instead, I made her wash off the marks on the wall and, the way she hates to work, this was worse to her than a beating.

In practice, however, Mrs. Martin was constantly threatening to "beat your butt", and frequently did beat the children. One of the things she would whip them for was fighting among themselves. She said that they were worse inside the house than they were outside. She did not want them to fight each other; if she let them, they would "tear each other apart". Dorothy and Brenda were the main offenders. When I asked her what she did to stop them from fighting, she said, "I beat both of them and don't tell them nothing."

Mrs. Martin gave the impression of being a spirited, aggressive person who made no bones about the position that "ain't nobody gonna tell me nothing". As if in imitation, both Dorothy and Brenda were aggressive. Mrs. Martin both condoned and complained about the characteristics they shared:

> I don't ever tell them not to fight, but I tell them not to hit first. It's bad to mark up another child. They gets a beating for that.

> Dorothy has got a bad temper. . . . Sometimes she comes all the way home from the playground to get a stick or something to hit somebody. She will mark you if you let her. She scratches.

> When I see her sucking her thumb and saying nothing, I know that she's in a bad way and ready to fight.

> I guess I marked Dorothy. My sisters used to hit me, and I would throw things at them. I would pick up anything I could get. . . .

Three-year-old Brenda had no hesitation in tackling children older than herself. She would challenge a boy as quickly as a girl. When I commented on Brenda's readiness to fight and to retaliate for seeming slights, Mrs. Martin said, "I tell her about that. I tell her she's going to get hurt one day if she doesn't leave people alone."

On a rare occasion when Brenda did run to her mother complaining that a child had hit her, Mrs. Martin cupped Brenda's face in her hands and said firmly, "Have you forgotten you got two hands? Go push her back! I guess I'll have to do something to you, because you forgot you got two hands. You better not forget!"

It seemed that when Mrs. Martin was not threatening to beat her children, she was warning them of some dire fate. On one such occasion, when Brenda was climbing up the wire screening of the patio, Mrs. Martin shouted:

Come down from there! You will fall and break your head open and all the blood will run out and then the boogey man'll get you!

Seemingly unimpressed, Brenda continued up the screen. *Providing the basics: priorities and realities.* Naming the things that she thought were important to children, Mrs. Martin said: "Food, clothes, medical care, a mama and a daddy."

Unlike Mrs. Todd, she gave priority to food rather than to rent. During my stay in the project, I witnessed one of her crises involving the basic necessities in which a food problem loomed large. I was a direct participant in this crisis, as I was in other incidents.

Mrs. Martin's husband had not been making the court-ordered support payments regularly. Since she had been using her $80 monthly supplement from the Welfare Department primarily for food, she fell a month behind in rent payments. She managed to borrow one month's rent from her father when she received a dispossess notice, but, by that time, two months' rent was required. After she paid the rent for two months, she was left without money for food.

She reported her financial difficulties to the Welfare Department and was told that nothing could be done until the following month, June. Her husband would have to be taken to court first, and this would take some time.

Confronted with this rule and response, Mrs. Martin sarcastically said, "And what am I supposed to do? Starve in May?"

To complicate her financial problems further, Mrs. Martin's two-year-old daughter, Tootsie, had just returned from a hospital stay for treatment of pneumonia. The doctors said her illness was due to the lack of proper food. Mrs. Martin understood and did not try to evade the doctors' diagnosis. She pointed out that she did not have enough money to feed her children properly, much less to buy vitamins.

When I offered to help, she accepted. I was again in intimate contact with hunger.

Mrs. Martin decided first to apply to a welfare agency for emergency help in getting food for her family. After unsuccessful attempts to make satisfactory, workable baby-sitting arrangements in the project for her four children, she suggested that we take a chance on finding one of her sisters at home. Taking the children with us, we traveled to a different section of the city. We found her sister at home and willing to look after the children.

Leaving the children with her sister, we drove to an office of the welfare agency. Despite her apparent brashness in many areas, Mrs. Martin was fearful of going into the agency's office alone because she had never been there before. She wanted me to accompany her; with a little encouragement, she went in by herself. We agreed to meet at the car; I told her I had some business of my own to attend to elsewhere.

When I returned from my errand, Mrs. Martin was already in the car. She sat slumped dejectedly in the corner. Her agency mission had taken only a few minutes. She had been told immediately that she could not be helped without a referral slip from her public assistance caseworker.

I gave Mrs. Martin a dime to call her caseworker. After the call, Mrs. Martin returned to the car, disappointed again. She said that her caseworker promised to call the welfare agency but told Mrs. Martin she could not see her until the following day at which time she would give her a referral slip, provided the welfare agency agreed to help.

Annoyed at this delay, Mrs. Martin said that if her caseworker had had any consideration she would have called the welfare agency while she was near the agency, especially since she knew Mrs. Martin's plight. A good bit of her annoyance was due to her hunger. Before entering the agency's office, she had wistfully expressed the hope that the agency would be serving sandwiches; she had heard they did this. However, there were none.

After she had given her account of the agency visit, I asked what food she had at home. She had some chicken backs and rice for the children's dinner. She remarked, "That will do them for tonight as they are not bad; they understand the situation and know that I don't have anything." As far as the next day was concerned, she said, "I'll just have to let tomorrow take care of itself." It was then I let her know I would provide food to tide her over until she found out whether she was going to get help from the agency.

We returned to her sister's house for the children. As we drove up, her sister called from the window to ask if Mrs. Martin wanted some herring. Mrs. Martin's quick rejection of the offer surprised me. It developed that the herring was part of their father's fishing catch of the day before. He had already brought some to Mrs. Martin, but the fish had been too bony for the children.

Mrs. Martin's sister came down to the car with the children. In her hand was a large brown paper bag which contained day-old bread that her boyfriend had brought from the bakery where he worked. Mrs. Martin's face lighted up as she thanked her sister and told her that the children had just eaten the last pieces of bread before we left. I witnessed this scene: Mrs. Martin had poured syrup on a slice of bread for each of the three older children who folded the bread, sandwich style, to eat it. Brenda, the lively, aggressive one, bolted hers down quickly and grabbed the last piece of bread on which she poured more syrup. Then Dorothy and Tootsie clamored for more bread.

Mrs. Martin pleadingly and tenderly asked them to be patient, she explained that she was trying to get some food for them. The children quieted down. Seeing and hearing this led me to return to my apartment for some apples to take with us on our trip to the agency.

After our return to the project, I took the Martins enough food for the next morning. I found the children seated around the table eating syrup sandwiches made from the day-old bread their aunt had just given them.

The next day Mrs. Martin told me that she had not been successful in getting help from the agency. The reason she had been given was that the agency's funds had been exhausted in helping the unemployed.* Neither would she be able to get additional help from the Public Assistance Division until after the court hearing of nonsupport charges against her husband—a month away.

Mrs. Martin said that her friend, Mr. Tompkins, was due to make his $16 contribution the next day, and she was sure she could count upon him. In the meantime, she thought she could get some help from her oldest sister. She telephoned this sister and briefly explained her predicament. After she finished talking with her sister, she said excitedly that her sister had said that she would "fix me up if I come over".

This time search for food took us to a public housing project in still another part of the city. We took the children with us.** After we reached the sister's house and the sister went to the kitchen to pack the food, Mrs. Martin seemed deliberately to refrain from intruding; she confined her attention to her nieces and nephews, all of whom seemed quite fond of her.

Once in the car, Mrs. Martin could contain her curiosity no longer. She began rummaging through the box of food her sister had given her to see what was there.

"I hope she gave me some meat," she said wistfully. "Yes! There's some hamburger," she answered. "She always has hamburger."

Gleefully, she enumerated the other items as she discovered them. "There's tuna fish, bread, puffed wheat, shredded wheat—but where's the sugar? There's no sugar! I wonder what she expected me to put on the cereal? I guess she forgot."

When we returned home I took Mrs. Martin some sugar. She was unpacking her box of food and the children were again eating syrup sandwiches.

I checked with her the morning after the baby's father was expected to bring his money contribution. He had

---

* This was during a particularly harsh, snowy and cold winter during which building construction was at a standstill for prolonged periods.
** On the way Mrs. Martin confided that she was closest to this sister, much closer than to her mother. Her sister was a warm, friendly person, the wife of a serviceman and the mother of five children.

brought it. The Martins were breakfasting on eggs and scrapple. While Mrs. Martin and I talked, Brenda hurriedly finished her breakfast. Then she eyed her mother's half-finished plate of food and asked for more.

"Don't you be asking for my food!" exclaimed Mrs. Martin in mock anger, sensing Brenda's intent. "What do you think this is!" In predictable fashion, she continued, "Give me your plate. You can have some."

As Brenda handed her mother her plate, Dorothy began crying, "I want some too," and with this, Brenda tried to snatch her mother's plate for herself. Holding securely onto her plate, Mrs. Martin pulled it away from Brenda and divided its contents between the two girls.

"I never get to have my breakfast!" she grumbled.

Mrs. Martin used the $16 brought by Mr. Tompkins to stock up on baby food, milk, staples and meat. When asked how far the money went, she said that by the time she had made these purchases, she did not have enough money left to get all the vegetables she needed. When I gave her some vegetables, the food crisis was over, for a while anyway.

Mrs. Martin wanted to repay me in some way, just as Mrs. Todd had wanted to do. I gently but firmly discouraged her idea of buying a present for me when she received her public assistance check. It was hardly a surprise when, on the day surplus food was distributed, Brenda appeared at my door with a half pound of butter her mother had sent me.

Getting an education: "to get out of the kitchen". Mrs. Martin took pride in the fact that four of her five brothers and sisters had finished high school. The one who had not was a brother who had been a habitual truant. Ticking them off with satisfaction, she said, "One of us is in the Police Department, one is a beauty shop operator, one is at Woodward and Lothrop's, and one is a housewife to a serviceman."

Many times she said that she wanted her children to do well in school and go as far as they wanted.* Her pre-

---

* The expressions "as far as they want" and "as far as they can" appear quite frequently in CRS materials in reference to parents' wishes and expectations for children's school careers.

ference would be to see them study nursing or get a government job, but, "I'll be satisfied as long as they ain't doing no day's work in anybody's house and working in anybody's kitchen!"

Mrs. Martin took advantage of the half-day, preschool program and showed excitement and pleasure in anticipating Dorothy's starting kindergarten. But, like Mrs. Todd, she was worried about how she was going to clothe the girl adequately and properly. She was very thankful to her sister who worked at a department store for buying Dorothy four school dresses.

V

ASPECTS OF RECREATION AND LEISURE

The Lack of Fun

The lives of some of the mothers had been surprisingly restricted despite their lifelong residence in the city. Just as some spoke of not having had any childhood, some spoke of not having had any fun, either as children or adults.

Mrs. Todd, for example, did not attend her first movie until she was 17 years old. It was only after Helen (the young lady who lived with me) failed several times in efforts to involve her in discussions of recent movies and movie stars that Mrs. Todd was moved to explain her lack of knowledge about them. "Don't ask me about any movies unless they've been on television as those are the only ones I know," she told Helen.

She said that she had never gone anywhere as a youngster, and that the only reason she finally got to go to the moving pictures when she was 17 was that she had to take her younger brothers and sisters with her.

The situation was not too different with Mrs. Queene, who

had grown up in the southeastern section of Washington but was a stranger to the central city. She said that when she was younger, she went downtown so seldom that unless she came out of the same door of a store that she went in, she had a hard time finding her way home.

"Would you believe it?" she said, "I was 17 years old and didn't know where 8th and K was."*

Mrs. Queene's father used to call her a dunce for not knowing where different places in the city were, but her mother blamed Mrs. Queene's father for their daughter's ignorance of the city, charging that he never let the children go out. Although he had a car, Mrs. Queene claimed that her father never took them anywhere. "All he did was keep his car polished and sitting in front of the house full of gas," she said.

After I had been acquainted with Mrs. Queene for a while, I invited her and her children to join my family on an outing. I asked if she had ever been to the Nature Center in Rock Creek Park; she responded, "You won't believe me, but I've never been to Rock Creek Park! I told you, I've just never been anywhere!"

We visited the Nature Center, the zoo and one of the playgrounds in Rock Creek Park. The outing pleased her so much that she made a plan to have her husband take her back to the park the next Sunday.

I happened to see her husband the following week, and he greeted me with, "Say, will you tell me how to get to that playground in Rock Creek Park? I drove 67 miles last Sunday trying to find it and never did!"

Once Mrs. Queene told about a friend of hers who had married an older man. She quoted her friend as saying that the difference between her age and that of her husband was unimportant; she was ready to settle down because she had had her fun. "That's something I can't say I have had," she observed.

Mrs. Queene wanted very little by way of recreation. According to her, she would have fun bowling or going to see the stage show at the Howard Theatre once a week with her husband.

* A transportation-exchange area near the main downtown commercial center.

Many of the mothers and fathers stayed at home or did not venture too far out of the neighborhood. Small children and the lack of money rated high as restraints. They must be counted among the reasons why television was the most common form of entertainment for both the young and the old.

Elderly Mrs. Harris timed her departures from the court to coincide with the start of the television programs she looked at regularly. She would say, for instance, "I wouldn't think of missing 'Ozzie and Harriet'."

Mrs. Queene was a soap-opera fan. She and her friends were so engrossed in the plots and happenings of the daytime serials that their discussions of them had the quality of talk about real-life situations. They would frequently have lively discussions of the pros and cons of some actor's behavior, and they would fill each other in on episodes that any of them had missed for one reason or another.

The cartoons on television were a must for the small children. On any late afternoon or early evening I could find Mrs. Todd's four children lined up on the sofa intently watching the cartoons. Generally, whenever Mrs. Todd left the children alone, she left the television on. The ways in which Mrs. Todd and other parents used television in child rearing indicate that some parents felt greater security when they had to leave their children alone because they thought television helped keep young children out of mischief.*

Mrs. Todd and her neighbor across the hall, Mrs. Norris, made working the crossword puzzle in the Washington *Daily News* a joint part of their respective morning routines. They kept their apartment doors open to make it easier to walk

---

* This coincides with a succinct evaluation of television made by a father who lived outside the project. Although his wife had spoken disparagingly of the low intellectual level of many television programs and said she preferred that her children not see the bulk of them, he did not hesitate to praise television as "the world's best baby sitter". Undoubtedly, among the reasons for the frequency of television sets among low-income families both inside and outside the project are its baby-sitting and mother's-helper functions.

and talk back-and-forth as they discovered new words and encountered problems.

Mrs. Todd was expert as well as avid; the harder the crossword puzzle, the more challenging it was to her. After she found out that I liked to work crossword puzzles, she began to bring puzzles over and we frequently worked on them together. She knew many of the uncommon words demanded in some crossword puzzles and kept a notebook of unusual words in anticipation of future need. Sometimes she would pore over the encyclopedia she owned in search of a word and, at other times, she would borrow a dictionary from me. We developed the kind of bond that is common among crossword puzzle fans.

Card playing was another favorite indoor activity of the parents with whom I was in continuous contact. The games played most frequently were "tonk", "pitty-pat",* pinochle and bid whist. (Contract bridge was not among the games I saw played but one or two mothers did express an interest in learning the game and this led me to some speculative questions.)**

The interest we shared in card playing provided another bond between Mrs. Todd and me. Mrs. Todd was a very good card player. At the time we came, she had begun to get bored with beating Mrs. Norris at "pitty-pat". Helen and I provided a new challenge; she would get together with us whenever possible to make up a foursome for bid whist. As time went on, she would bring friends and relatives to play. It was on occasions such as these that she came to life and showed a zestful capacity for enjoyment that one might not have expected.

* "Tonk" and "pitty-pat" are variations on *tonque*. They are popular among working-class and rural segments of the population.

** For example, how to explain the apparent lack of interest in, or lag in knowledge about, contract bridge on the one hand, and, on the other hand, the evident interest in, and up-to-date knowledge about, fashions and fads in dress and home furnishings. The answer seemed to lie in the fact that the latter could easily be picked up from the popular magazines but learning contract bridge required a teacher. My offer to give some lessons was readily accepted, but I was not able to find the time to do so.

Monopoly and bingo were other games that interested some of the mothers with whom I had contact. Record playing was also popular and the frequent exchange of records made it possible for friends to hear each other's latest acquisitions. Negro recording artists were the general favorites. To get a hi-fi set was a common wish, and many had one, even though the set might be one of the cheaper portable models.

Mrs. Todd eventually bought a hi-fi set on the installment plan after some frustrating postponements. When she finally got it, she would spend hours lying on the sofa and listening to records after she had put the children to bed.

Get-togethers and parties were frequent and usually were impromptu gatherings of six to twelve people to play records, dance and drink.

Mrs. Doyle, one of The Girls who lived on the floor above me, used to complain that the people who lived across the hall from her would start a party on Friday night that lasted until Sunday. Although, once in a while, I heard other parents complain about noise and late parties, I was never disturbed by them. My impression was that late parties were the exception rather than the rule.

One aspect of the get-togethers and the partying that especially interested me was the manner in which the supplying of drinks was handled. Although, on occasion, a host or hostess might have a little liquor to get a party started — or to dole out to special friends — it was the usual practice for a guest, especially a male, to bring some liquor; a half pint was in order.

If the liquor supply was running out and if the party was "still going strong" after the liquor stores had closed, people at this kind of party would chip in nickels, dimes and quarters to get another pint or half-pint from the local "bootlegger".

The word "bootlegger" took me by surprise since I had just come from the South where the bootlegger's commodity was moonshine. But this was not the case here. The "bootlegger" was a useful middle-man; he purchased standard brands of liquor at a liquor store and resold them at higher prices when the liquor stores were closed.*

This practice is an illustration of kinds of adjustments and inventiveness one is likely to find among low-income people. Parties with dancing and drinking are characteristic of all levels of our society. While presumably higher status and more affluent hosts are able to—or are constrained to—provide drinks for their guests, the low-income host and his guests cooperate in an acceptable mutual aid arrangement which could not work without the "bootlegger".

Entertainment Away from Home

Visiting relatives in other parts of the city ranked high among the away-from-home, leisure-time activities of these families. Although some of these visits to relatives provided changes of pace and scenery, my impressions are that they could not always be called entertainment. Mrs. Queene, for example, went to her grandmother's every weekend, sometimes to let her grandmother take over the children for a while and sometimes to cry on her grandmother's shoulder about her marital problems. There were always some signs of conflict when Mrs. Todd visited her parents, but one of the satisfactions of the visit for her was the likelihood of a good card game.

Church-sponsored outings, especially in the summers, were frequent; many families would take part in at least one during the season. These church-sponsored affairs were advertised by placards, church announcements and word of mouth. They included boat rides down the Potomac River, picnics, and trips by chartered buses to nearby resorts and cities, as well as to places that were up to two hundred and more miles away—for example, Hershey, Pennsylvania; Wildwood and Atlantic City, New Jersey

* When I asked Mrs. Todd why people would pay "bootleg" prices when they could get whiskey at the store for less, she informed me, with what I felt was a tinge of disdain for a "square", that the "bootlegger's" rates were no higher than those for liquor at a nightclub. She did not add that a weightier reason might have been that it was easier to chip in on a bottle at any price than to buy a bottle oneself.

and Coney Island.*

Fishing was another popular leisure-time activity of some of the male and female tenants. I would see successful fishermen coming in with strings of fish and sometimes witness the sharing of their catches with other tenants. Mrs. Queene and her husband used to go fishing on one of the branches of the Potomac River. She regretted that these outings had ended when her husband bought a used car and began frequenting taverns instead.

Going to taverns and nightclubs was a must for some of the younger people, particularly the men. One of Mrs. Queene's major complaints about her husband was that "he spends all his time in taverns", a trait that she disliked intensely.

Once, in commenting on tavern experiences and hazards, Mrs. Queene said:

I'm not no goody-goody girl, and I've been in Washington all my life but, would you believe it, I've never been inside a night club!

One time I went with my husband to one of those taverns and there was a fight and a bottle just missed my head. Another time there was an argument, and someone brought out a gun. When I saw the gun I started running. My husband tried to tell me that the thing for me to do was sit still because if I ran they would think I had something to do with it. But who wants to stay around when someone has a gun!

Once in a while, one of Mrs. Martin's sisters would take her along to a nearby tavern for spare-rib sandwiches and beer. This was a prized treat for Mrs. Martin since she seldom got away from the project. Sometimes the young people, including Mrs. Todd and some of her girl friends,

* I went on one such picnic with Reverend Nelson's church to a Negro-owned-and-operated beach on Chesapeake Bay. The beach was small and crowded. The drunk and the sober, the loud and the quiet, the religious and irreligious were confined side by side, so to speak, in this extension of a Negro working-class ghetto.

traveled to night clubs on H Street, NE, and, more rarely, to night clubs on U Street, NW.

The clubs boasted a live combo and a tiny dance floor where patrons performed the latest dance crazes, for example, the "Madison", the "Mashed Potato", the "Pony", the "Twist" and their variations.

The athletic activities of the recreation center attracted many, particularly the men, and there were also the dances sponsored by the center.

I attended one of these dances with Helen, Mrs. Todd and Mrs. Norris and found the guests to be mostly young people in their late teens and twenties dancing to records. I found that times had not changed too much from my day for there were the girls grouped on one side of the hall and the young men on the other.

Thinking that I was only going to be an observer, I found, much to my surprise, that the young men, closemouthed though they were, were not averse to dancing with a gray-haired lady, for more than one silently proffered his hand. It took me a little time to get used to the fact that this gesture was not followed with, "May I have this dance?" Nor was there any conversation while we danced unless I strained to make it. My partner's abrupt departure at the end of the dance leaving me on the floor, social amenities aside, seemed to be the general custom of the young generation in this setting.

The Children's Fun

Numerous statements by mothers, in particular Mrs. Todd, Mrs. Queene and Mrs. Martin, pointed up their desire to be able to provide more fun and recreation for their children. Statements in this vein kept cropping up while I lived in the project.

The beach party for the children that Mrs. Todd dreamed about has already been referred to. It took a little effort on her part to settle for a lesser outing with only cold sandwiches to eat. She and her children went with me on their first trip to the beach to Sandy Point, a public beach and state park in Maryland.

Mrs. Queene did not waver in her determination to make Sunday a family day. She would frequently express longings to go on an outing with the family, and she would specify various places she had read about or had heard about.

Even in the midst of some acute crisis because of lack of money for food, Mrs. Martin did not forget about her children's entertainment. When, after considerable delay, she got some money to take care of basic physical needs, she held out a dollar for the carnival the recreation center was having; she wanted to see her children ride on the ponies. On the Fourth of July she supplied fireworks for her children, and our two families shot Roman candles and lighted sparklers together.

VI

YOUNGER CHILDREN AT PLAY

Informal Rules and Aspects of Play

My observations of the children's play were probably made easier, and certainly sharpened, by the fact that I had a four-year-old son. Watching him play with other children made me more conscious of some aspects of young children's play in the housing-project setting than I might otherwise have been. I was particularly struck by two features of play behavior among the young children: the need to learn to hold one's own and the delayed development of play skills.

Holding one's own. I had looked forward to letting my son play in the court while I kept a watchful eye on him from the window. As soon as he knew his way, I let him go to the court alone when he asked.

After he made a few such trips, I began to notice he was

reluctant to go to the court, and that he wanted to play in the house or in the hall play area. This shift made me curious since it was unlike him to want to remain indoors when he could be outside.

My repeated suggestions that he play outdoors were eventually countered with his statement that he would not do so unless I went to the court with him. After this, I went with him when he went to play in the court. As I watched the children at play, I began to understand why he was reluctant to go to the court by himself. The play was rougher than he had been used to; he did not know what to do other than to retreat.

On one occasion I watched a boy about eight years old follow my son, who was riding his tricycle, and suddenly give him a hard push on his back. Richard pedalled furiously trying to outdistance the boy who kept up with him on foot and continued to push him. Not sure what the trouble was, I headed toward them and could see the tears streaming down my son's face. When my shouts at the boy attracted his attention, he darted into the apartment building and did not return to the court. Richard had no explanation for the boy's behavior and had never seen the boy before.

My own speculation was that the boy's behavior had something to do with my son's having his own tricycle. Some children would ask for a ride on the tricycle, take a brief turn and return it. With others, Richard would have a hard time getting the tricycle back after letting them have it. Once I saw a child walk up to the tricycle, grasp the handle bars and edge him off the seat without saying a word. On a different occasion I saw another child, apparently without provocation, approach from behind a child who was riding Richard's tricycle and hit him with a stick.

These instances were not the rule, yet a few such experiences as these had apparently convinced my son that he preferred the lesser hazard of playing in the house or in the hallway. It was clear to me that he was faced with a new situation, different from the protected nursery-school environment to which he was accustomed. There were no teachers and aides to turn to; he had to handle the situation himself.

Observing what the other mothers in the court did, I noticed that they taught their children to fight back.

Characteristically, when a child came to one of the mothers in the court crying about having been hit, the mother showed little or no outward sympathy for the tears. In most instances, she would demand to know why her child had not hit back or retrieved the toy that had been taken. Whatever the case, mothers seemed to be making the point to their children that they should respond to attack or to slight more aggressively. A mother was likely to send her child back into the situation with such advice and a threat of punishment if he did not obey her instructions.

At the same time the mothers were insisting that their children learn to protect themselves, they also tried to curb their children when they were the aggressors. For example, some would exclaim irately, "Didn't I tell you not to do that!" or, "You know better than to do that!" This was often followed by a few resounding wallops and a promise of more to come if the behavior continued.

The intent of the mothers seemed to be on teaching their children some of the harsh lessons of survival. In this sense, the court, the playground and the streets are frequently grim, informal and effective educational settings for low-income populations. The fact that children have to learn to hold their own was nothing new to me. What was new was that they were learning to do so at the ages of two and three.

Soon, I was involved in similar counselling of my child.* I found that I even had to soft pedal sex distinctions, since the girls were frequently as aggressive in play situations as the boys. Illustrative of many children, but not neces-

* Before long, my son was reporting pridefully that he had hit some-one back and had not cried. I have no doubt that when we moved he was further along in holding his own with other children than he would have been had we not lived there, and I must confess my pleasure at seeing him wind up on equal footing with a few of the children from whom he had initially cowered.

My own thinking was that my son was at the least none the worse because of these experiences. His pleasant memories of these 15 months have been evidenced on the several occasions he has expressed a wish to return to play with his former playmates in the court.

sarily typical of all, was Mrs. Martin's three-year-old Brenda, who could fight as well or better than any boy her age and did not hesitate to tackle children older and larger than herself.

One byproduct of some of the children's play and conflict was feuding between their parents. Certain children were tagged as "bad" and some mothers warned their children not to play with them. Some of the more protective mothers did not let their children play in the court because of their fears about the aggressive behavior of some of the other young children.

Lack of developed play skills. My observations of the children at play left the impression that many of the children had not had the stimulation and opportunities for sustained imaginative play.

I saw this lack when I watched John and Jim, four- and five-year-old brothers. They were very close; I never saw one without the other in tow. They made their way independently around the project and the nearby area, almost like two against the world.

They struck up an acquaintance with my son in the court; Richard's automobile, in which they delighted in riding, helped seal the bonds. Soon they began coming to the apartment almost daily. On John's first visit, he discovered my son's toys and excitedly called out to his brother, "Come see! He's got a whole closet full of toys!"

As time went on, it did not really matter to John or Jim whether or not my son was at home so long as they could get in and have access to his toys. Their relationship was essentially with the toys, and my son found it almost impossible to break through their preoccupation with a toy to involve them in imaginative play. They were content just to push a fire engine around the room dinging the bell, while my son would try in vain to get them to pretend there was a fire and to build a play situation around the fire.

Soon my son's interest in John and Jim dwindled. He had lost them to his toys, at least temporarily.

Although I did not know their family situation, my impression was that John and Jim had fewer toys than many of the other children I saw in the court; I never saw them bring any kind of toy into the court as some of the other children did. In speculating about the behavior of John and Jim, I thought that, at least in part, it could be attributed to their lack of playthings.

The possibility that there was a direct relationship between no toys to play with and the lack of developed play skills did not provide a complete answer, however. I observed a similar unresponsiveness to imaginative play in children who were well supplied with toys, such as Mrs. Queene's son. Consequently, I came to think that it was not necessarily the possession of toys that stimulated a different level of play.

I continued to watch my son's relationship with other children and noticed that the boys in whom he showed the greatest interest were the ones with whom he could develop and carry out imaginative play. Apparently the fact that these boys were always two or three years older than my son had some significance. In these instances this age differential appeared to have no relationship to whether the children appeared dull and slow, or alert and bright. The two boys specifically mentioned here appeared alert and bright.

I thought that the lack of imaginative play among some young children might be related to the absence of family and extrafamilial situations conducive to learning and developing play skills. It was clear that the opportunity to develop play skills was affected by some of the child-rearing consequences of living poor. Let me elaborate:

When I arrived my son was already in his second year of full-time nursery school where he had been learning and developing play skills under trained personnel. Although he was more advanced with respect to play skills than some of the children in the project his age, the same children tended to be more advanced in other respects.

While he had been learning play skills in the nursery school, the children he came to know during these fifteen months had been learning how to hold their own. He was learning the ABC's of cooperative play while many of his playmates-to-be were learning the ABC's of survival in conflict.

A number of mothers who have participated in the Child Rearing Study have said that they had had no childhood. This perception of an important lack is reflected in Mrs. Todd's comment that she had been a mother ever since she was 12 and in Mrs. Queene's speaking of having nothing to look back to. The early assumption of adult roles seems to have been the fate of many project children and parents. Life in the housing project tends to demonstrate that the pressures of low-income urban living and family size often rob some children of much of the encouraging support and direction and many of the opportunities for developmental play.

VII

YOUNGER CHILDREN'S LANGUAGE

Variability in Speech and Vocabulary

Problems in language were quite evident among a number of the families I knew. I was puzzled that in some instances, even within one family, there was marked variation in the speech patterns of its members. Mrs Todd's family was an example.

Elsie, Mrs. Todd's five-year-old daughter, had fluent speech, good enunciation and a sizeable vocabulary. Her speech was in sharp contrast to that of her four-year-old brother Phillip.

Phillip had trouble with the enunciation of many beginning consonants, both single and double. He called a fire a "pire" and a truck a "twuck". In addition, he stuttered.

Mrs. Todd made attempts to help him. Occasionally, she would try to get him to practice the correct pronunciation of a word but would quickly give up in despair when he repeated his mistakes. Mrs. Todd seemed to concentrate on learning his speech mannerisms and translating all his errors. She could always translate any of his expressions that someone else did not understand. This may explain why his sister and brother understood him quite well.

I had difficulty, at times, in understanding Phillip, but improved under Mrs. Todd's teaching and example. My son was less fortunate and it was obvious that frequently he felt quite frustrated in trying to understand Phillip. The language barrier probably meant that their relationship was not as close as it might have been.

Phillip's three-year-old brother Nicholas did not speak as poorly as Phillip nor as well as Elsie. On the one hand, he had some of his sister's fluency and, on the other hand, he had some of his brother's trouble with consonants. However, he was always understandable. The fourth child in the family, nine-month-old Shirley, seemed to be developing normally in learning to talk. Mrs. Todd put considerable effort into teaching her new words, and she was learning them quickly and correctly.

My neighbors, the Norrises, had a different kind of speech problem in their three-year-old son Ronald, the youngster that held me so tightly when I picked him up. He used a kind of fluent gibberish that was like a foreign language interspersed with an occasional word in English. When Ronald spoke, he would look up at me earnestly and searchingly, as though he were hoping to find some sign of understanding. From his intonation I could distinguish sentences, questions, and even paragraphs. Sometimes I heard a simple word like "car" or "train" and often his gestures would give some clue as to what it was he was talking about. Whatever he was saying seemed to have coherent meaning to him. Occasionally he would pause as though waiting for an answer to one of his questions or for a comment on something he had said. Now and then he would laugh after using some choice word or expression that was beyond question uniquely his own. Although he struggled to communicate, even though he could not be understood by others, he could understand them well.

Mrs. Norris, who had a lisp, acknowledged that most of the time she did not know what Ronald was talking about. The only explanation she had for his speech was that he might have gotten it from her because she becomes almost speechless when she gets excited.

Another person with a lisp was Mrs. Martin's four-year-old daughter, Dorothy, who was also a thumbsucker. Dorothy was the only one of Mrs. Martin's children who had a speech problem.

Mrs. Queene's five-year-old daughter had excellent speech, but her four-year-old son was still having trouble with beginning consonants and talked in a babyish manner.

The language difficulties observed suggest the probability of an unexpectedly high incidence of untreated and, in a sense, unnoticed speech problems among both children and adults in the poorer segments of our society.*

Absence of Speech Consciousness among Parents

In trying to think about some of the language problems I observed, I kept returning to what struck me as an absence of speech consciousness among some of the parents. For example, the speech of the three mothers to whom I have devoted a considerable portion of this report was replete with grammatical errors; yet they had been educated in District of Columbia schools and each had had at least two or more years of high school.

Usually, their major language errors involved subject-verb disagreement: "He do", "I tries", and "They be's".

There was a puzzling inconsistency in this pattern of speech error that led me to think that among some mothers it might be due to carelessness rather than to a lack of knowledge. Sometimes the mothers made these errors, and sometimes they did not. In general, there seemed to be a lack of concern about grammar; they never corrected themselves when they did make mistakes.

The attitude of these mothers toward their own speech habits probably accounts for much of their children's poor

---

* This is written with full realization that some of the complex social, psychological and economic factors related to language development and use—not to mention physiological, genetic and other factors— are beyond the scope of this report, although some of the former have been alluded to.

and erratic speech. I never heard any of the mothers I was acquainted with correct her children's grammar. A very common grammatical error among children was in the use of pronouns: "Me want to go with you", "Her hit me", or "Him did it".* Even though the parents themselves did not make this mistake, they overlooked it in their children, along with their errors in subject-verb agreement.

This type of speech error in children, and the accompanying lack of correction of such errors by parents, were recurrent among many of the low-income families observed by the CRS field staff. This behavior could hardly be attributed simply to a mother's lack of interest in her children; it existed among some of the mothers in our study who had the widest range of interests and most intense concerns about their youngsters. Poor and erratic language behavior in children and lack of corrective behavior in low-income families are undoubtedly functions of a number of factors, of which income is but one.

Many low-income parents themselves seemed not to have experienced anything different with respect to language behavior when they were children. I heard some of the same errors in the speech of their parents and relatives that I met. It seemed that the acquisition of language skills had low priority as compared to acquisition of food, shelter and clothing.**

Although the mothers described did not correct their children's grammar, they did correct their children when they used profane language, even though the children may have heard their parents use such language. Watchfulness against children's use of "bad language" did have a high

* These are understandable mistakes in the very young child learning to talk whose concept of himself and others is still on the "me" and "him" level. But one does not normally expect to hear four- and five-year-olds talking like this.

** This low priority may be related to the fact that so many of the jobs to which low-income families are accustomed are ones that do not require language skill. Working in service and laboring occupations does not require a knowledge of grammar and syntax. Undoubtedly many families have not built up the same kind of orientation toward the attainment of language skills that a white-collar family has. Seemingly people cultivate the language, as well as other tools, that have proven necessary.

priority. During these 15 months I never heard a child use "bad language" in the vicinity of his mother without being corrected.

It appeared to be more important to many parents to try to see that their children did not pick up "the language of the street" than to try to see that they spoke grammatically. Our field observations suggested that some, not all, CRS families were so tied up in dealing with gross immediate survival problems that they never got around to dealing with the refinement of language. This does not mean that most of these parents were necessarily unaware of the practical and esthetic values of "talking good".

Another paradox related to the language problem among low-income children is suggested by my observations of the studiousness with which Mrs. Todd taught her youngest child new words in contrast to her failure to correct her older children's grammatical errors.

It seemed to me that there might be a parallel between Mrs. Todd's behavior with respect to her children's learning to talk and the way she had put Shirley down once she had learned to walk. In other words, once some parents had helped a child to learn to walk or talk, the child was on his own to fend for himself. Teaching words and phrases was important for communication but grammatical construction was not.

At times I speculated that among the reasons some parents did so little about the language of children was that they saw language skills as something a child would learn when he got to school. Many appeared to have little awareness of how engrained a child's poor speech habits could become by the time he reached school age.

A question which deserves much more probing is the effect that the amount and quality of communication between parents and children have on the development of language skills. It seemed to me that among the poorer project and nonproject families, the preponderance of communication between parents and children was about behavior and basic physical needs, areas which involved considerable repetition of commands, admonitions and prohibitions.

There seemed to be more and better communication between mothers and daughters than between mothers and sons. This may have had something to do with the fact that, generally speaking, the girls I knew had better language skills than the boys.

My residence sensitized me to another language question that is worthy of much more probing than I was able to undertake, namely, the relationship between language problems in a child and his ordinal position. In the families of Mrs. Todd, Mrs. Norris and Mrs. Martin, the child with the language problem had been followed by another in a year. Having to make way for another child just at the time verbalization is beginning may have adverse effect on a child's language development, both in terms of decreased communication with the child on the part of the mother and the possibility of emotional blockings in the child as a result of the new arrival.

VIII

LEADERSHIP AND COMMUNICATION AMONG THE POOR: SOME ADDED COMMENTS

For me, living as a participant observer under the circumstances described required a delicate balancing of professional detachment and intimate involvement. The interplay between the two helped to sharpen my sensitivity to some of the anomalies in the lives of many of the contemporary urban poor.

Indications of some of my gropings for perspective on what it means to live poor in an urban community in the early 1960's are scattered throughout this report. Some of these reflections bear on current concerns about the poor and on programs to benefit them. Some afterthoughts that grow out of this particular field experience have to do with child rearing, the economics of living poor, efforts to develop leadership among the poor, and communication with the poor.

Afterthoughts on Mothers and Children

I brought to this field experience, as a member of the Child Rearing Study staff, somewhat conventional notions about the behavior and characteristics of the "good mother", and the inclination to think that certain lacks, or some not-too-well defined combination of lacks, identified the "bad mother". I found it necessary to reassess some of my thinking about the mother's function and status in some of the types of low-income families I got to know. My perspective on (or appreciation of) low-income parental behavior began to change.

Gradually, I realized that my preconceptions about, and my initial reactions to, the child-rearing performances of some of the mothers were quite different from these mothers opinions of child-rearing jobs they were doing. Their self-ranking was relatively high, even though, like Mrs. Todd, they could not always meet the standards they set. The favorable self-ranking among these mothers seemed to be related to the fact that they thought they had made, or intended to make, an advance over the child-rearing behavior of their parents.

The childhood experiences of some of these mothers, who had themselves been reared in poverty, seemed to have left a strong, persistent sense of shame and indignation because as children they had to live without many material and nonmaterial things. Their effort to provide "something different" for their children, more food, more clothes or more affection, had a much greater significance than I had at first surmised. They showed an insistent, although not always consistent and focused, design to do more and better for their own children than had been done for them by their parents.

I began to see how some urban mothers who are poor

ranked various aspects of child rearing and became aware that their order of importance of various child-rearing demands and needs was probably different from that of adequate-income mothers. If I were ever tempted to be judgmental about these mothers who sometimes seemed to see their children's needs more in physical terms than in psychological terms, I had only to think about what lay behind the comment of one young wife and mother who, in trying to reconcile herself to her family's circumstances, said, "After all, you have to crawl before you can walk."

As I learned to judge these mothers in terms of where they saw themselves on the child-rearing performance scale I became able to resist any temptations to overstress and overgeneralize negative traits. I developed instead an approach geared to getting better understanding of their reasons for their child-rearing priorities.

The usefulness of knowing how mothers who are poor see themselves is suggested by the following experience:

A social-welfare consultant was interested in getting the reaction of some mothers to the draft of a pamphlet that was being prepared to introduce special playground equipment for young children that was to be installed in a play-area program. It contained a discussion of the importance of play prepared by a specialist in pre-school education and included some statements about the responsibilities parents would be expected to share in supervision of the play area. I showed the pamphlet to several mothers.

Some of the mothers could not understand why the material on play had been included because it was "the same kind of advice on how to raise children that they tell us everytime we go to a meeting anyway".

Others felt that the pamphlet was not written in terms that applied to them. Mrs. Todd made two comments. First, she pointed to the use of the singular "child" throughout the booklet and added that it "did not sound like it was written for parents with three and four children" because there are things that can be done with one child that just can't be done with three and four. She also pointed to the pamphlet's emphasis on the importance of a child's having "his own toys" and said that some parents cannot provide "own toys" and have to teach their children just the opposite—to share.

Some mothers saw evidences in this material of "talking down" and of failure to recognize some of the actual problems and pressures experienced by so many low-income families with several children.

The Economics of Living Poor

The cash that could be counted on by the families I knew was severely limited; they had to count every penny. Their money was earmarked and overclaimed before they got it. They had more things that needed to be done, and that they wished to do, for family and home than money to do them with. Harsh choices among efforts at satisfying basic needs and unfrivolous wants had to be made and lived with constantly.

A Mr. Queene, for example, might decide that he would rather try to buy a used car than furnish the additional bedroom they were expected to take but which his wife felt they did not need. A Mrs. Martin might prefer to let her rent go unpaid in order to feed her four children, and a Mrs. Todd might feel impelled to pay her rent rather than feeding her children adequately. Choices among limited alternatives tended to be individualized decisions made by each parent or set of parents. For each family I knew, there was always more than one insistent claim on each dollar of a very meager supply of money. The precarious gap between income and claims on it is not unique to the low-income family. But the poor have to spend a significantly larger proportion of their income on basic necessities.

As I got to know and to absorb a great deal about the daily routines and the physical and social contexts of the lives of many parents and children, the logic of many of the choices and much of the behavior of these low-income families became clearer. It became easier to understand a man like Mr. Queene who worked on cars all day and wanted one for himself—even though perhaps he really could not afford it—or the anguish of mothers like Mrs.

Martin and Mrs. Todd who did not willingly let their children go hungry and would not willingly see them and their belongings set out on the street. From my vantage point, many choices appeared neither irresponsible nor callous. Some seemed particularly poignant. All appeared related to compelling demands and issues of the situation, if not the moment.

The families I knew and observed established child-rearing priorities in their own ways. It appeared that what was deemed of first-ranking importance was related less to any fundamental differences in life standards or goals for children than to the lack of means. And sometimes there was evidence of the father's and mother's lack of confidence in their ability to meet and sustain standards expected by others whose means are different.

It was not always possible for the poor parents I knew and observed to reflect in child-rearing and other behavior all of the standards associated with the middle-class way of life even though many saw these standards as being desirable. "To get ahead" was an important desire among several of the families I knew, particularly the younger ones, and it had been a driving force among some of their parents and relatives.

On Leaders of the Poor

Most of the low-income people we have come to know in various settings have an underrated sensitivity to the behavior of others and a kind of built-in ability to estimate the seriousness of people and the effective chances that real change will occur. As one mother said of her illiterate husband: "He ain't got no education, but he's sure got mother wit."

Participant-observation experience led me to realize that there are some big differences between the ways in which many low income people see and regard themselves and the ways in which they are seen and regarded by outsiders. This is one reason why the recent rash of allusions to the indigenous leader need to be examined, as well as the assumptions and thinking from which it stems. Webster defines "indigenous" as, "Born, growing or produced naturally in a region or country; native". It is in this sense that the term is used in programs of aid to the so-called underdeveloped countries; the indigenous leader is seen as bridging the language and culture gap between the foreign expert and the population of the country. However, currently in this country, the term is being applied to certain residents of local neighborhoods. Most frequently, these residents are members of racial and nationality groups and are presumably representative of the lower class.

To many low-income people, the term "indigenous" would make no sense, and to others it would be offensive and alienating in the manner it is now applied.

If we see the low-income people who live in certain sections of our American cities as indigenous to a particular area or as bearers of a different culture (when it is highly doubtful that the areas or cultures are as different as usage and assertion indicate), we are committing, wittingly or unwittingly, descriptive and labelling errors that endanger our efforts to help urban poor people and to help them help themselves. For example, rarely, if ever, do we hear of an indigenous middle-class leader of the suburban stripe, except possibly in a facetious vein.

Another danger in the loose use of indigenous in contemporary settings where low-income families live is that it leads to false assumptions about what people want, and underestimations of their ability to assess accurately their needs, wants and what they get in promises and services.

The following instances caused me to examine more closely what people want as compared to what others think they need:

When Reverend Nelson visited me to express his interest in my becoming assistant Sunday school superintendent, I think he came because he saw me as a person with some training, and this meant to him that chances were good that I had some abilities and knowledge that would help him achieve what he wanted for the children in his church and in his neighborhood. It was this "know-how" that he felt I had, and that he did not have among his church leaders, that was probably the important consideration in his design for change.

When Mrs. Cartwright asked me to join her church because she felt "the Lord had work for me to do there", she too was probably stimulated by my "nonindigenous" qualities. She said it would take the conversion and help of people with educational background and socioeconomic status to bring her church the respect and recognition she thought it deserved.

Both Reverend Nelson and Mrs. Cartwright were asking for competence and experience not present in their current situations.

Living and working with low-income families reinforced my impression that most low-income people, like most other people, have respect for, and prefer, competence.

Qualities considered important for a leader would include competence, accessibility and acceptance of the local residents. These are probably more important than whether or not a person is "indigenous to the group". For some kinds of problems, being a local resident and having these qualities is likely to prove a boon; for others, whether a person is local or not may not matter.

On Communication with the Poor

One of the presumed assets of the indigenous leader is his ability to "speak the language" of his neighbors or group. For example, many current references to "speaking the language of the poor" come to mind, but no one seems to have defined just what this language is. A part of the problem comes from the tendency of some to make a narrow and literal application of "speak their language". This tendency appears to be based on the assumption that communication is relatively impossible without an intermediary.

Opposed to this narrow and limited view is the tendency to see and apply the broad connotations of "speak their language" as social scientists, and other professionals do, for example, in the sense of "getting inside" a group or community. In these instances, direct communication and understanding are considered a professional responsibility.

My impression is that, to some people, this "language"

is the vivid colloquialism of the exasperated mother who tells her child she is going to "bust his hindparts wide open"; to others, it is the profane remark or the sex-tinged allusion that slips easily from some tongues; to still others, it connotes the limited vocabulary or the ungrammatical speech of the untrained, the careless and of those to whom it no longer matters how they sound. And then there are those who believe the poor to be essentially inarticulate.

After listening to members of a large number of low-income families, I have no conviction that it is necessary to speak in any of these terms in order to be understood or to get along.

The language of those affected by poverty is frequently simple, and, like poverty, it is often stark. But, it can also be mixed with subtleties and nuances, and these can be caught if one listens with patience. In many situations, both public and private, the language of the poor is direct, graphically expressing the needs and demands of life— sometimes more direct and grating than a person might care to hear. Yet, there is rarely any mistaking the meaning.

Poverty, more often than not, does not foster niceties of language any more than it fosters the development of social graces. The problem is not one of having to speak a different language but of being willing and able to listen to what is said and to respond with respect and sincerity.

In the Child Rearing Study, we found that it was readiness to listen and to understand that opened doors. That we were able to understand what we heard was affirmed in a direct fashion by Mrs. Todd.

Handing a newspaper clipping to me, Mrs. Todd said, "This is about you." And then she stood silently looking out my living-room window, with her back toward me, as I read the article. It was a report of a paper read by a staff member of the Child Rearing Study at a national professional conference. The news feature bore the headline:

*"They Strive for Middle Class Standards but Often Fail
A Problem of the Poor—Frustration"*

I read the article with trepidation. I had never anticipated so direct a confrontation. Gingerly, I began an interchange:

"Did you read it," I asked.

"Yes," she said.

"What did you think about it?" I continued.

"It's true," she said laconically.

"Are you talking about any particular part of it?" I inquired.

"All of it," she replied.

"What do you think about the different explanations he gave?"

"Stop talking!" she responded quickly.

"I've answered you," she added. "You talk too much. Don't give me any more lectures!"

Among parents in general, but probably to a greater extent among parents who are poor, much behavior that is called apathy is understood better as "knowing the score". The child-rearing choices, and other choices made by the low income parents observed during the field operations of the Child Rearing Study struck me as reflecting impressive grasps of the "score" of the life situations in which they found themselves and of themselves.

Rather than language impediments that restricted communication, I found feelings of acute loneliness and isolation in many poor parents. These feelings were likely to respond to a sympathetic ear and to a demonstration of interest. For example, my early relationship with Mrs. Martin led her to tell her sisters about me even before they had met me. In the same way that her grandmother did, I apparently afforded Mrs. Queene an opportunity to blow off steam. She said of our association and conversations, "It helps me. It gives me a chance to get things off my chest, not just about my marriage, but about other things that have happened even before that."

For Mrs. Todd, our relationship had an even deeper meaning; it was reflected in her gradual use of the term "mother" in connection with me.

When I told her I was moving to another location, she said dispassionately, "I wish I was leaving." But her next question was, "How many bedrooms are you going to have?"

I told her how many rooms I would have and asked why she wanted to know. She replied, "Because I want to see if you have enough room for me!"

Mrs. Camille Jeffers, Associate Professor in the School of Social Work at Atlanta University, received her bachelor's degree from the University of Illinois, a certificate from the New York School of Social Work, and her M. S. W. degree from Atlanta University. She is presently developing a special student field instruction unit in a public housing project under the auspices of the U.S. Children's Bureau. Her background includes social work in public and private agencies in New York, involving work with the blind, the aged, dependent and delinquent children, the armed forces, merchant seamen, trade unionists, displaced persons, and minority groups. During World War II, she served two years with the Red Cross in England and, after the war, worked with the United Seaman's Service at the National Maritime Union. Her experience also includes service on the Intergroup Committee on New York Public Schools while she was employed by the Urban League of Greater New York.